Lost

With All Hands

A Family Forever Changed

by

Mary Melton

PENOBSCOT PRESS

This book is dedicated to my mother, Emily Brown Stone, whose stories of her Down East seafaring people take us back to a time when vessels were moved by wind in the sails, men were at the mercy of mast high waves, and cemetery monuments read, "Lost at sea."

Contents

Introduction

This is the story of the Portland Gale, the greatest maritime disaster in New England's history, and its impact on seafaring families in Down East Maine.

On Saturday, November 26, 1898, most of the men who earned their living at sea were out on the water. Relatives who had gone to Boston for the Thanksgiving holiday were expected to return Sunday morning on the steamer *Portland*. The 281-foot sidewheeler left Boston's India Wharf at 7 p.m., filled with people bound for Maine.

A warning telegram to those engaged in transportation had come from the Washington weather bureau that morning, and red flags were hoisted in coastal ports from Norfolk, Virginia, to Eastport, Maine. The telegram warned of northeast gales and heavy snow, with wind shifting to the west and northwest.

Some coastal sea captains, in port when the telegram came, decided the warnings didn't sound worse than weather conditions they had dealt with many times, and went on their regular runs.

No one foresaw the possibility that two major storms, one coming up the coast from Hatteras, the other across country from the Great Lakes, would collide over the Mid-Atlantic and begin moving north. No one could even dream of the fierceness of such an encounter. The snow was thick and blinding, the wind so strong that people were swept off their feet; waves became 30 and 40 feet high.

The *Portland* was lost, with no survivors, on Sunday, November 27, off Cape Cod. Bodies began washing ashore around 3:30 Monday morning. Because of the great number of people who'd been aboard this ship, nearly 200, the storm was given her name.

During the weekend of November 26 and 27 an enormous number of vessels were lost at sea between New Jersey and Nova Scotia, with the brunt of the storm in southern New England. Some authorities believe 400 vessels were lost with more than 500 people. No exact count is possible because small vessels were splintered in the storm, and neither parts of boats, nor bodies of the crew, washed ashore.

Families in a number of small Down East villages found themselves cut off from all news. Telephone and telegraph wires had been downed in the storm, and 10 to 12 foot high snow drifts prevented the mail from getting through.

The wait for news was an agony. When the mail finally got through, the screaming headlines above lists of sunken ships and lost loved ones, was worse than anything they could have imagined.

Prologue

November 7, 1898

A cold wind blew across the busy I.L. Snow shipyard at the edge of Rockland's crowded harbor.

The new captain stood at the edge of the high bank, the stem of his pipe clenched between his teeth. His damaged two masted schooner, the *Addie E. Snow*, sat inside the marine railway cradle.

From the nearby roundhouse, he heard the steady clop from the hooves of four horses. As they circled, they shortened the heavy cables attached to the cradle.

His dark eyes never left the vessel as the cables pulled the supporting structure onto tracks that went down into the water at a steep incline on big timber. The protective device had been fastened to heavy iron bars on top of the tracks, and rollers fit onto the bars. Once on level land, the encased schooner rolled slowly along the marine railroad.

The new captain ran a thumb and forefinger back and forth along the width of his luxuriant red moustache. "Rotten luck," he said aloud. "I should be aboard her, bound for New York."

He'd passed his tests just a couple of weeks ago, and had been put in charge of the *Addie E.* on November 1. To become a sea captain meant everything to him...always had. He wanted to follow the long-time traditions of his seafaring family, and lead the adventurous life of his grandfathers, uncles, and older brothers.

Up until the first of the month, an older brother had been her captain and he'd been mate. He had been aboard her on many runs up and down the Atlantic Coast, as well as on several passages to the West Indies.

He'd been given the *Addie E. Snow* as his first command when the shipyard owners had transferred his brother to the three masted *Robert A. Snow*.

When on a misty morning, he had steered the *Addie E.* out of Rockland Harbor, a heavy fog had moved along the Atlantic and enveloped the schooner, a fog so thick he could see nothing beyond the bow of the schooner. He heard the warning fog bells and whistling buoys, and desperately tried to steer clear of the rocks, but with a sickening thud and a great lurch ran aground on Placentia Isle. The rudder and the after plank of the hull were stove up so bad, she had to be towed back to the yard for repairs.

Such accidents were not uncommon, and he'd been held blameless, but because of being a new captain, it had been a great embarrassment. He wished he hadn't bragged to his friends about his new position. Were they laughing at him now?

The young captain saw a swarthy, full bearded ship's carpenter watching the progress of the vessel. "Eli," he said, "can you give me an idea of how long she'll take to repair?"

The fellow moved his chew to the other side of his mouth and spat on the ground. "Ayuh. About a week and a half, Cap'n."

As the cradle rolled slowly over the shipyard's marine railroad tracks, Percy turned to look out into the harbor. Vessels called Johnny Wood Boats were bringing cord wood in from down Nova Scotia way for the great lime furnace built into a man-made hill, well behind the wharves. The vessels were built with very square noses so they could bring more wood than other schooners.

Horse drawn wagons loaded with limestone rattled into the yard. Men in old clothes, and with untrimmed beards, loaded the stone into the cars of a small train which spewed cinders as it climbed the trestle leading to the top of the huge furnace. They dumped the contents into its roaring wood fire, which burned at high heat day and night, turning rock into lime.

At the A.F. Crockett lime wharf, casks of lime were being loaded into the hold of the schooner, *Robert A. Snow*, bound for New York and due to leave with the tide. Her master had his 17-year-old bride aboard.

Anchored farther out in the harbor was a "Snow" vessel which didn't look badly burned from the outside, but the inside was beyond repair. The fire had begun in heavy weather, with the schooner on her beam ends. Waves washed over her, flooding the hold. Casks overturned, a lid came off, and a deadly mix of salt water, lime and oxygen had started the fire. The inner parts of the schooner had to be closed off to contain the fire, and the men had to stay on deck in below zero weather. They arrived at the next port almost frozen to death.

The young captain could see his brother standing on the quarterdeck of the *Robert A. Snow*, giving orders, his voluptuous wife beside him. When the brother glanced toward shore, the young captain gave him a "thumbs up" for good luck on his run to New York. Because the vessel was carrying lime, he wished the seas weren't so rough, but his brother was a talented player in this game between man and the sea.

On Saturday, November nineteen, the young captain steered the newly repaired granite schooner *Addie E. Snow* into East Penobscot Bay. As far as the eye could see were dozens of rocky, spruce covered islands. When he looked into the distance, the wild and lonely scene made him think it must look the way it did hundreds of years ago. He half expected Penobscot Indians to walk out of their woods and come rowing toward the schooner in birch bark canoes.

Standing on the quarterdeck, the young captain felt the burn of the wind on his face. At nearby islands, white capped water kept the fishing boats at their moorings. At several of the nearby islands, other granite schooners rocked in the water.

They arrived too late to begin loading, and no work would be done on Sunday. "Heave to!" he ordered when they reached a lee shore off St. Helena Island.

The mate shouted the order to the deck hands. At the mate's direction, anchors at both bow and stern were let go into the choppy water, and the sails were furled.

On Sunday all was quiet except for the sound of the surf against the schooner and the cries of the seabirds flying overhead. The young captain stayed in his cabin for much of the day. He read from the book, *Two Years Before the Mast*, and wrote a letter home.

The deckhands were whittling out Christmas gifts. Both of them worked on heart shaped jewelry boxes. The mate, who had children, concentrated on a board game, with a many jointed wooden man who would dance when a child pulled the strings. In the late morning, the cook cut himself and came to the cabin for Opeldock Salve and a bandage from the medicine chest. When the wound had been treated, and the young captain bent to close the wooden chest's dark cover, with its gold scroll work around the name ADDIE E. SNOW, he thought how pretty it was.

Monday morning, when assaulted by the screech of the stone cutter's drill, Percy reached into the medicine chest, pulled scissors from one of the leather loops at the back of the cover, and cut some pieces of bandage to stuff into his ears. Through the following days, the island men loaded the hold with granite paving stones at a slow pace.

"Norwegian steam," the mate commented sarcastically.

The young captain watched carefully as the men placed the paving stones in the hold, and secured them. On the afternoon of the twenty-fourth, he judged the hold to be filled to capacity, in terms of safety. "That's all she'll take," he said in a firm voice. The men selling the stone argued with him that a few more wouldn't make any difference, but he didn't give in.

He didn't want the same thing to happen to him as had to one of his older brothers. Two and a half years ago, he had sailed from another of the granite isles, carrying paving stones and bound for New York. After a week of storms, the stone in his overloaded schooner, had worked loose in the hold, the pumps had broken, and the schooner, in sinking condition, had to be abandoned at sea.

The daylight was fading into grey, and Percy knew he'd have to wait for the morrow to start his run to New York. He decided to sail as far as Seal Harbor, about 30 miles, and leave the next day with the tide. That evening, beneath a kerosene lamp that swung overhead, he studied his charts and read from his book. Before extinguishing the light, and climbing into his bunk, he glanced toward his brother's gift, a carved model of the *Addie E. Snow*, presented when the new captain had been given command of the vessel.

Lulled by the rhythm of the water, and on the edge of sleep, his last waking thought was of thankfulness for the great life that lay ahead of him.

On November 25, the *Addie E. Snow* left at noon with the tide. The schooner, heavily laden with granite paving stones in the hold, and some secured on deck as well, traveled low and slow in the water.

She passed the twin lights on Metinicus Rock almost in the center of the approach to the Bay, then the God-forsaken Saddleback Ledge Light.

As the short, wintry day merged into darkness, and a high wind and slashing rain overtook them, the young captain decided to anchor that night in Portland Harbor. "No sense in taking chances," he said to the mate, who nodded in agreement.

The next day, Saturday, November 26, the *Addie E.* sailed out of Portland Harbor under clear skies and with a fresh breeze. "We'll make good time today," the new captain said. "Aye," the mate replied. "That we will."

In the middle of the afternoon, however, the wind stopped blowing, and as the schooner ceased to move ahead, a strange bronze light filled the sky. Bad luck, the new captain thought. A humdinger is on the way. But without wind to move the sails, there was no way to reach safe harbor.

When at last the strange light faded from the sky, the twilight of a winter's evening began, and as a harsh wind picked up along the North Atlantic, the *Addie E. Snow* began to move again.

Snow started to fall, and, as the wind grew stronger, it blew the canvas cover off the hold. The new captain knew he now had to stay far from land, for to be dashed upon a rocky shore in a gale is the dread of every seafaring man.

Waves washed over the deck, fore and aft, and the *Addie E.* seemed to sink lower into the sea. He tied himself with rope to the wheel. Icicles hung from his red moustache and eyebrows.

Both masts broke, making great cracking sounds as they fell. They beat against the side of the schooner.

"Man overboard!" the mate cried, as one of the deckhands was swept into the raging black sea. But there was no way to help him.

Chapter 1

The Village of Walpole, Maine

Zena

Zena Brown lay sleepless in the four poster bed, while her red haired husband, Joe, snored peacefully beside her. Although she had drifted off several times, visions of storm tossed ships had repeatedly jarred her awake. In her last attempt at sleep, a hand reached up for help through black, white crested waves. She shook with a sudden chill. Was one of their sons at sea in danger?

In the flickering light from the bedroom hearth large photographs of their six children, looked out from elaborately carved and gilded frames above the mantel. The two girls were pretty; and the four young men, with their stylish moustaches, were all captains of coastal schooners.

Percy, the youngest son, had become a captain just a few weeks ago, on the first of November. She was proud of him, but the timing, right at the edge of winter storms, couldn't have been worse. Then the North Atlantic became fierce and cruel—one of the most dangerous places in the world—a hard season for even the most experienced of captains.

It would be easy to let worry take over her life. Just an hour or so ago a new day had begun. It was now Saturday, November 26, 1898, and she would try not to fill it with fear. But in spite of her resolution, she couldn't help but wonder where the boys were and if they were in danger.

Joe moaned in his sleep. She pushed her dark hair back from her face, took a careful look at him, and put her slender fingers on his forehead. He seemed to be all right—no fever. Although he had recently lost an eye to cancer, he was still a good looking man. In his youth he'd been the handsomest fellow in Lincoln County, a romantic figure, as he rode through the countryside in his doeskin shirt and pants, astride a white stallion.

The fire was going out, and a winter chill from the Damariscotta River blew in around the window frames. Zena got up, and hurried across the cold floor boards, past the hand hewn bureau and the door that led to the kitchen. Along the wall at the foot of the bed, she passed the wash stand with its white pitcher and bowl, before coming to the fireplace. She stooped to put several more sticks of wood on the hearth. As she turned back toward bed, she glanced at the door leading to the tiny room where she'd given birth to all their children, and where, long ago, Joe's mother had given birth to him.

When she lay in bed again, still too uneasy to sleep, the moonlight came seeping in. She turned her head toward the far side of the room where above a scarred sea chest which sat on wide floor boards, a window faced close by hemlocks and pines. In the wall near the head of the bed, another window framed a starlit view of fields and forest. Along the river, at the bottom of the ridge, a tall pointed fir stood silhouetted against the full moon.

In the little front hall, the grandfather clock struck twice, and Zena heard it, as she had all the hours and half hours of the night. Overcome with weariness, she at last felt herself relax.

Outside in the moonlight, the small white house and weathered barn atop Wawenock Ridge looked serene, but in the shadows at the edge of the woods a panther crept on padded feet—one of the big cats that each autumn came down from Canada, following its prey.

Suddenly the barking and growling of a dog in the farmyard, then the high pitched scream of a panther, like the scream of a woman in childbirth, brought her fully awake.

Joe rolled out of bed in his long underwear, and grabbed the shotgun standing in the corner. "Dad gummit critter's after the stock," he muttered. Bumping into the wash stand, then the chair, he opened the bedroom door and limped across the kitchen, past the pantry, into the summer kitchen, and toward the side door.

The creature's scream took Zena back in an instant to when she had been a young girl running home at dusk along the woodroad. Close beside her were heavy crashing sounds as a great animal bounded through the dense underbrush. She ran until she thought her heart would burst, fearing at any moment to be caught in the animal's great claws. But as she reached the trail that led to the house, there stood her home-from-sea father, his shotgun in the crook of his arm. He caught her as she fainted.

Two shots echoed in the night. Seventeen-year-old Josie came running down the stairs from her bedroom, her auburn hair flying, and mahogany colored eyes wide with excitement. "You missed him, Father. I saw him in the moonlight. He jumped the fence at the back of the barn. Ran into the woods."

"Wouldn't have gotten away if I'd had two good eyes. Didn't get lined up right."

Josie pushed strands of long hair away from her pretty face. "I'm going upstairs and watch out the window again. I'll get the spyglass

Josie Brown

out of grandfather's sea chest. I'll shout if the panther comes back."

"If he does, it'll be his last time," Joe said as he climbed into bed.

"When I heard that scream," Zena said, "it took me back through the years to when—"

"Lord, Zena, I've heard that story a hundred times." He rolled over, turning his back to her. "I'm going to Damariscotta in the morning. Got to get my rest."

"I wish you'd wait, Joe," she said. "It's too soon after your surgery."

He didn't answer.

She lay awake, frustrated and wounded. In past years, when she'd trembled at the sound of a panther's scream, he'd held her close, and they'd gone to sleep in each others' arms. But since January 6 of last year, their marriage hadn't been the same. Did he blame her for what happened? Did he blame himself? He wouldn't or couldn't talk about it.

Could it be that there was another woman, younger and more attractive, and she was the last to know? Zena didn't think of herself as pretty, but some said she had an unusual beauty—her features and coloring were a blend of European and Abenaki ancestry.

On thinking about the possibility of someone else in his life, Zena really didn't believe it, because before the tragedy they had been deeply in love. Now, even though he lay beside her, she felt a deep loneliness for him and for his touch. If he'd never loved her, if he'd married her just to have someone to take care of his mother, as some jealous girls said, she wouldn't feel this abandoned. But he had been so much in love with her that she had seen it in his eyes and heard it in his voice.

It had been a beautiful May morning, soon after their marriage. The chores had been done, and Zena was fixing breakfast. Joe's mother, Prudence Fitch Brown, sat at the table, across from her son. Zena filled their plates with fried smelts and potatoes, then brought squares of johnny cake and a half pound of butter molded with a fancy floral design on top. "More tea, Mother Brown?" She reached for the pot, kept ever-warm at the back, right hand side of the woodstove, just beyond the firebox.

"Don't need a thing, child," Prudence said, her blue eyes glowing with affection. "You sit down and eat."

Suddenly a hoarse shout came from beyond the side door. "You there, Mr. Brown? You there? It's the weir. She's full of alewives. There's thousands of them."

Joe stood up fast, knocking his wooden napkin ring to the floor, where it rolled under the table. "Come on in," he hollered, and hurried past the pantry and into the summer kitchen.

The door banged back against the wash tub, and a barefoot young man rushed inside, clay clinging to his feet, cut-off trousers, and tattered apron. "You've got to see all the fish in the weir, Mr. Brown. There's thousands of them jumping in the water. I left the kiln and ran up here. Thought you'd want to know."

"Thanks, Horace! It's great news."

The young man was one of those who worked in the family's brickyard. It seemed as if just about everyone along the Damariscotta River had one. He stayed a couple of minutes talking to Joe about business.

Zena, who had been to the waterfront several times with Joe, could imagine how it had been down there at first light. One of the brickyard workers would have called out to come quick. They'd have stood along the river bank staring out at the circle of spruce stakes, its nets filled with silvery fish moving in the roiled water. Only the night before, her new husband had complained that the weir caught so few fish, and the nets were so expensive, he might have to give it up.

When the workman left, Joe dashed back to the table. "Come on, Zena. Let's go look." He took a big mouthful of smelt and fried potato, then quickly wiped around the borders of his moustache with his napkin. "When those alewives are sold, I'll get me a new farm wagon, and I'll get you a whole bolt of that blue China silk."

"A whole bolt?" she'd said, laughing.

He had yanked on the strings of her blue and white checked apron, but as it fell she'd caught at the waist band with her long, slender fingers. She glanced toward his frail mother. "Maybe I oughtn't leave...."

"You young folks go along," Prudence said. "Don't worry that I'll get up and fall. I won't move till you get back."

Zena had snatched her little shoulder shawl from a nail behind the door, then as Joe pulled her outside, she glanced back. His mother had fixed her eyes on the great painting above the fireplace. There, her husband's favorite ship, the *Barque Noble*, sailed on forever through white capped water, the great square sails catching the wind.

Painting of the BARQUE NOBLE that hung above the mantel.

"Come on, Zena," Joe had said, and holding hands, they ran outdoors under a bright blue sky, where fluffy white clouds floated lazily, unmindful of the young couple's urgency to witness the near-miraculous. Beyond the planted fields, the cows grazed placidly in the upper pasture. Glimpses of the Damariscotta River showed between the tops of tall pine, spruce and fir trees at the bottom of Wawenock Ridge.

At the edge of the upper pasture, the newlyweds had changed directions and headed toward the mile long lane at the far right. They ran down the wide path, through the hundred acre forest set off for Prudence when she married, by her father Jonas Fitch, a captain in the Indian Wars. On either side some red oaks and white birch could be found, but mostly fragrant pine trees, spruce, and balsam firs.

Zena and Joe had kept on running, past the ruins of two houses built at different times by his ancestors. From near the fallen structures, pink and white apple blossoms showed between the evergreens.

Zena slipped on the thick evergreen needles underfoot, and nearly fell, but Joe caught her. As they ran on, she took pleasure at the sight of the ferns and mosses growing at the edges of the lane, and of a variety of wildflowers: jack-in-the pulpits, lady's slippers, and violets both purple and white. When she'd had to stop for a moment to catch her breath, Joe had picked a dark green stem of sweet smelling pink-white mayflowers and stuck it into her thick dark hair.

Zena wondered if Joe would ever love her again. It had been a year and ten months since the tragedy. The husband of a friend, whose adored daughter had died, had never recovered from the loss—never again showed his wife affection. From the little front hall, the grandfather clock, brought home in the *Barque Noble*, struck three. She thought of the many times they had heard it strike through the night as strong winds screamed along Wawenock Ridge and heavy sleet pelted the windows. They'd been unable to sleep for worry over the boys, whose heavily laden coastal schooners were out in raging seas.

They worried, too, during the boys' not infrequent passages to the West Indies, taking clapboards, pipe staves and lumber to Baracoa, Guadeloupe, and Monte Cristo, and returning with cotton, indigo, and molasses. She and Joe were uneasy because hurricanes could arise quite suddenly in those tropical waters, or cyclones which began far out at sea and raced toward land, whipping the ocean into a frenzy.

Zena said a prayer for Lemmie's safety on his way home from the Caribbean, and the Spanish War. Then very weary, she felt herself drifting off.

She heard Josie's voice, as if from a distance. "Mother, wake up. Mr. Owen's walking this way. Coming to see you."

Zena opened her eyes barely enough to see Josie's pretty face.

"Did you hear, Mother? Mr. Owen's coming."

Zena, her eyes now wide open, sat up in bed, her long black hair cascading over her white flannel nightgown. "Why so early?"

Josie laughed, cupping a hand over her mouth. "It's nine o'clock."

Zena pushed back the covers and swung her legs over the side of the bed. "Nine o'clock? I've never slept this late!"

"Don't worry, I finished all the chores. Made the tea—even started the baked beans."

"If you aren't the limit!" Zena said, smiling fondly at her daughter.

The tall, slender girl in a white shirtwaist and floor length black skirt moved gracefully toward the kitchen. "I'll get you some warm water," Josie said over her shoulder. She reached for a tin basin and a dipper, kept on a low shelf, and began ladling water from the reservoir at the right hand side of the woodstove.

Anxious to be ready before Mr. Owen arrived, Zena hurriedly pulled on her long sleeved under vest and tights, and added a wool underskirt against the late autumn chill. She reached for her black dress, with the white linen collar and cuffs, until recently her Sunday best.

Mr. Owen visited several times a year when he caught a head cold and was afraid he was going into pneumonia. She could picture the small man with the thin grey beard, almost lost in a too-large suit and overcoat, hand-me-downs from his stout son, Hiram, a Boston lawyer.

He was not without standing in the community, however. He was as well known for his ability to predict the weather as Zena was for her herb doctoring. With the next season right around the corner, she knew he'd tell what her boys could expect...a mild winter, she hoped.

Josie returned with the tin basin filled with warm water, and a cake of homemade soap. As Zena washed her face, she asked, "Why did you let me sleep so late?"

"Father said not to wake you."

Zena nodded, and smiled at his kindness. "He's in the barn?"

"No. He left for Scotty."

Zena drew a sharp breath. That rascal! Joe knew she would keep him from going so soon after his surgery. It had been just a couple of days ago—Thanksgiving afternoon—when he'd had a dizzy spell, fallen and twisted his knee.

"He didn't want to wait," Josie said, as she handed her mother a towel.

"I pray nothing happens," Zena said. While she pulled on her stockings and high black leather shoes, Josie combed out her mother's long, dark hair.

From outside, the young dog barked to warn of a visitor on the property. Mr. Owen must be starting up the rise of the front yard. Zena parted her hair in the middle from forehead to neck, arranged it in two three strand braids, and after winding them together, used wire pins to secure them in a pug at the back of her head. She took her small gold loop earrings from the top drawer. "Did your father take someone with him to help, in case he felt sick or faint?"

"Mr. Kelsey."

Zena gasped. "Simon Kelsey is blind and your father only has one eye, since the cancer took the other one. What if they have a bad spill? What do they think they can do?" She shook her head, puzzled. Joe wasn't a stupid person. He knew better than to take such chances.

Fully dressed, Zena stepped into the kitchen, and into the warmth from the big brick fireplace. Rays from the morning sun beamed through the front window. On the mantle a small ship in a bottle reflected its glow, while in the big painting above it, the great ship *Barque Noble* sailed endlessly off the southern coast of Portugal. The windows at the back of the room, one at either side of the woodstove, revealed a view of pasture, woods, and river, which she loved. But today there wasn't time to enjoy it.

As she reached for her black sateen apron, on a hook to the right of the stove, a knock sounded at the door.

"Helloo! Anybody home?" came a quavery voice.

"Come in, Mr. Owen," Zena called out as she tied the strings of her apron behind her back.

Once inside, he leaned on his cane with one hand, and against the wall with the other, overcome with a strangling cough. He wore a handsome, but too large grey wool overcoat and a suit of the same color. The too-long pants were raveled at the bottom, from being dragged along the ground.

"Run out of my medicine, Zena," he said when he caught his breath. "I'm afeared this bronchitis will turn into lung fever."

She took hold of his elbow to steady him, as he walked to the deacon's bench in front of the hearth. "I'll fix some white willow tea, while you're here," she said, "then give you a tin of the dried bark to take home."

"Hello, Mr. Owen," Josie said.

He sat up a bit straighter on the bench. "You've gotten mighty pretty, Josie."

A smile of amusement flickered for a moment in Zena's dark eyes. Men never saw themselves as old. She lifted her shawl from the back of the rocking chair, and threw it around her shoulders before entering the unheated summer kitchen where bunches of herbs hung from the rafters. A wooden box held her jars of dried and pulverized bark.

Returning with one of the jars, she put a teaspoonful of the bark into a squat brown teapot, then added a cup of boiling water. After it steeped for fifteen minutes, the tea would be just the right strength.

Josie piled a plate high with molasses doughnuts and set them in the center of the Turkey red oilcloth that covered the table. The old man stared in anticipation at the fried cakes.

"Have a bite to eat with us, Mr. Owen," Zena said.

He stood part way up, then fell back onto the bench. "Still a mite dizzy."

"Stay right where you are," Zena told him.

Josie passed the plate of doughnuts, and he took two. "Didn't have breakfast," he explained.

Zena, looking for the correct size tin in which to place the rest of the dried bark, signalled to her daughter to pull two chairs from the table to the fireplace. She and Josie could sit facing him, and he wouldn't have to eat and drink alone.

After following her mother's directions, Josie stepped into the cold cellarway for milk to add to their cups of Pekoe tea. The family teapot would sit all day the back of the stove, to the right of the firebox, the brew growing continually stronger.

When the willow tea had steeped for the allotted time, Zena strained it through cheesecloth into a cup and handed it to her guest. She placed a tin of the dried bark on the empty place beside him.

"Much obliged," he said. Holding the cup in both hands, he stared at her unblinkingly, his dark eyes alert in a sea of wrinkles. "Zena, this winter's going to be a screamer, and it'll start with a whoop and a harroo!"

She shivered with a sudden chill in spite of the heat from a brightly burning fire. Although her sons questioned his old-fashioned methods of weather prediction, which included fox fur and goose bone, she'd never known him to be wrong.

Vivid pictures of her children at sea passed through her mind. She saw darkly handsome Lawrence, aboard the three masted schooner *Robert A. Snow*, with his pretty bride Myrtie Belle, bound from New York to Salem carrying coal. She concentrated next on fair skinned, red haired Percy, aboard the two masted schooner *Addie E. Snow*, bound from East Penobscot Bay to New York, carrying stone. Then she saw Lemuel, Lawrence's identical twin, aboard the gunboat *Scorpion*, in his navy uniform, headed home from Cuba and the Spanish War.

The dog barked again, and hearing the sound of horses' hooves and carriage wheels, Zena looked out the front window, to see her full bosomed, well-girdled sister, Cretia, being driven into the yard. Mr. Walker, the hired man, drove the span of horses. He wore an old army hat, and his scraggly gray beard blew in the wind. In his left hand he held the whip at-the-ready; he'd wrapped the reins around the large steel hook at the end of his artificial right arm.

She recalled how her boys, when they were little, couldn't take their eyes off the hook. "How'd you lose your arm, Mr. Walker?" they would ask on every visit.

"Well, it were this way, lads," he had drawled in his deep mild voice. "Lost her in the War of the Rebellion. Just outside Donaldsonville, Louisiana it were. July 13, 1863...."

As Zena opened the door, Cretia called out, "I can't stop to visit. Got to get to the newspaper office before noon."

"Next time, then," Zena called back. Cretia was forever putting notices in the paper about her family's activities.

Josie grabbed her shawl from the nail behind the door, and ran out into the yard. "Hello Aunt Cretia and Mr. Walker," she said. "Any news?"

The plump woman smiled fondly at her niece. The hired man touched the brim of his hat.

"Your Uncle Frank and Aunt Delia are coming. They'll leave Boston tonight, get into Portland Sunday morning; come by train to Newcastle."

Zena partially closed the door and leaned her forehead against it. The mention of their names brought back sorrow.

"Something wrong, Zena?" Mr. Owen asked.

For the moment, she'd forgotten he was there. She couldn't think what to say. Then she seemed to hear her mother's voice: "Stand tall, child, and never show weakness."

"Just a touch of rhematiz," Zena said.

"Ah, I suffer from it myself," he said, and helped himself to another doughnut.

She shook her head to clear her mind. "My sister, Cretia, has come by. Might give you a ride."

"Sounds good," he said, his voice muffled by a mouthful of doughnut.

She opened the door again. "Cretia, Mr. Owen is here. Could you drop him off home?"

"We'll take him along now."

Zena nodded and turned to her visitor. "You've got a ride. While helping him into his oversized coat, she added, "Remember to strain the tea." Standing at the window, she watched through stick-like lilac bushes as the carriage moved up the road at a brisk pace. Until last year her view would have been blocked because of the tall hackmatacks, planted when saplings as a wedding gift from her parents.

Her brothers, as sweat rolled down their sunburned faces, and the muscles in their tattooed arms rippled, dug in the hard earth, then planted a row of trees down each side of the front yard from house to road. She recalled how each of the boys had, among other tattoos, one of an anchor, which was a talisman to prevent him from drifting away if he fell overboard. Her youngest brother, who had been ordered aloft in an ice storm, had the letters H-O-L-D F-A-S-T individually tattooed on his knuckles to protect him from falling.

Cretia's carriage disappeared between the trees that lined the road. On the way to Scotty it would wind through deep woods, and, occasionally, cleared farmland. Josie, who'd run down to the road, and stayed waving until they were out of sight, came shivering into the house, her face glowing with excitement. "I can't wait to see Aunt Delia and Uncle Frank! I can't wait!"

Zena could hardly bear to hear their names. Waves of strong emotion took her strength, and she sank into the old rocker by the window. She took a deep breath, then lifted her basket of mending from a small stand beside the chair. "I knew they were coming," she said, "but I disremembered when."

"They're sailing on the *Portland*," Josie reported. "Aunt Cretia says it's the most beautiful overnight steamer there is. Each ticket costs a whole dollar."

Those two spend money right and left, Zena thought.

"They'll stay at Uncle Eph's. He's planning a Stevens reunion next week."

"It will be too late in the fall to chance going to Pemaquid Harbor," Zena said. "If the winter snows begin we mightn't get back in time to milk."

"Mrs. Meyer goes there every week to see her father," Josie said. "Maybe I could go with her."

"Maybe."

"It wouldn't matter if I had to stay over a couple of days."

As Zena mended the toe of a heavy work sock, she thought about Frank, the younger brother she had loved enough to give her first born child his name. Growing up, Frank, handsome and mischievous, had been her favorite, and they'd remained the best of friends through the years. How unbelievable that on January 6 of last year her daughter May had died at his house in East Boston! She was just 16 years, 9 months and 22 days old.

Chapter 2

The Strange Bronze Light

Zena had been uneasy about letting May go to Boston in the first place. She remembered an end of summer night, just two weeks before their daughter planned to leave. She and Joe had gone to bed, but she couldn't sleep—just lay there worrying. She pulled the thin summer quilt up around her shoulders as a chill wind blew back the curtains. It came up from the river, and she thought it carried a faint smell of the fire from the brickyard kiln that burned day and night from May to September. From deep in the woods she'd heard a wolf howl, then several answering calls.

"I wish the teacher hadn't interfered in our lives, Joe," Zena said. "We had never thought of sending her to college. But Miss Cramer said May was a brilliant girl, and it would be a crime if she didn't go."

Joe sighed. "I was almost asleep, hon. I thought everything was settled."

"I don't feel easy about it," Zena said. "Boston is a wicked city. No place for a country person. My brother Mazina went there looking for work as a sailor and...."

In the moonlight that shone through the window, she could see Joe yawning. He'd heard the family story many times and had no interest in hearing it again. But it wouldn't leave her. The morning Mazina had left for Boston, carrying his duffel bag over one shoulder, all the family except the father had walked with him, down past the cows in the rocky pasture, to John's River. The brothers who were home from sea carried a rowboat upside down over their heads, the girls the oars, and their mother a basket filled with buttermilk biscuits, salt cod, and dried apple pie. His sisters had made penuche, and tucked the brown sugar candy in the corners of the basket.

Their father, home from sea for two weeks, was at the shore before them, sitting on a rock, smoking his pipe, ready to row Mazina out to deeper water, where the passenger boat to Newcastle would come by. As the rowboat was put into the water, the father had put a silver dollar into Mazina's hand. "In case of need," he'd said.

"We'll wait to hear," their mother said, giving him a hug and kiss.

But no letter came, and after awhile Frank and Eph had gone to Boston to try to trace him. When they showed the small daguerreotype, no one remembered him for certain, but a longshoreman who worked on one of the busy wharves ventured that he might have been shanghaied. On the same day Mazina would have arrived, a whaler bound for the South Seas, had been warped near the end of the wharf. He called her a Hell Ship no man would willingly sign onto. It was common knowledge that when a young sailor spilled tar on the deck, the captain had killed him.

The longshoreman also remembered a couple of crimps hanging about. They'd bought dinners for a few out of work sailors, then slipped knock out drops into their drinks. That night they'd been seen pulling a cart, with the drugged men in it, down to the Hell Ship.

"We never saw Mazina again," Zena had said aloud.

"Great day in the morning!" Joe muttered. "May won't be hanging around the waterfront. She'll be with Frank and Delia. With them looking after her what could happen?" He'd put his arm around her and within a few minutes she'd heard him snoring.

"Do you hear something, Mother?" Josie asked.

"Hark!" Zena said, putting a finger in front of her lips. "It's Uncle, across the river."

Josie ran through the kitchen, past the pantry, and into the summer kitchen, where she threw open the outside door. Zena, who was right behind her, picked up their speaking trumpet from where it sat on the floorboards.

"Joe..." he called. "You there, Joe?"

"Just Josie and I," Zena called back. "Joe's in Scotty."

"Don't like that. Henry just came from Scotty. He says red flags are up. Heavy weather coming. Hope Joe gets back soon. You two stay close."

Dreadful scenes raced through Zena's mind...Lawrence and Percy aboard heavily laden schooners in violent seas, great waves washing over the decks. She pictured Joe, weak and minus an eye, riding through a snow storm, with his blind friend. Too choked with emotion to shout back, she handed the speaking trumpet to her daughter.

"We'll stay close, Uncle. Thank you."

"That's all for now."

Zena shut the door, made her way back to the kitchen, and sank down into the rocker. Out of the corner of her eye, she saw Josie studying her, a concerned look on her face.

"Don't worry yourself sick, Mother," Josie said. "Lawrence and Percy will watch their barometers, then head for safe harbor. Lemmie's in the South Atlantic. Probably in good weather. Father's on dry land. He'll go to a house. Stay till the storm's over."

Zena bit her lip and looked out the window. The coming storm had to be the one Mr. Owen had warned her about. A storm that started with a "whoop and a harroo" would come on so fast there wouldn't be time to do anything, but try to survive. But there was no point in getting Josie upset. Trials aplenty would come her way as she grew older, the way they did to everyone.

"Let's think about happy things," Josie said as she opened the oven door to pour a little more water into the beanpot, "like seeing Aunt Delia. I love the way she laughs. And she always looks so pretty."

Zena pressed her lips tightly together. Why shouldn't Delia be carefree and pretty—a pampered woman who has never had a worry or sorrow in her whole life. Zena's sisters, Cretia and Euda, who live in Pemaquid Harbor, had told her that when Delia and Frank summered in their cabin along the river, he was so protective of her, she didn't even walk out to the backhouse after sundown, without him going along to wait there with the lantern.

Josie's eyes were dancing. "I think, Mother, that for the get-together I'll wear my silk dress with the tiny tucks in the bodice and the jet beads on the collar; and I'll have the new bertha I crocheted, to wear around my neckline. Oh, won't it be fun if the cousins and I can get Aunt Delia to tell fortunes with the tea leaves? She has such a gift."

Zena gave her thread a sudden yank. When May got sick at their place in East Boston, where was her "gift" then? If Delia knew so much, why didn't she see to it that Frank sent the telegram immediately, when the child's pain became severe and her fever high? Maybe if I'd gotten there sooner, the old time herbs might have saved her. Frank knew I had Indian cures that medical doctors know nothing about. He must have remembered how those time-tested medicines from the fields and woods had drawn out the infection and saved Lemmie's leg. He'd been injured so badly aboard his schooner that the surgeon at Boston hospital had wanted to take it off.

Perhaps May wouldn't have fallen ill in the first place if she hadn't worn herself out working at a factory, in addition to going to college. The child must have needed money badly, but was too proud to ask for help. Why didn't Delia and Frank let us know we hadn't sent enough with her? Joe and I had no idea how expensive college would be.

Zena hadn't known about the job until a letter from Delia said, "I'm making a lunch for May to take with her to the factory."

The night after the letter came—on January 4—a Friday, Zena had lain awake in bed, casting about in her mind for an answer to the money problem. It was then she remembered her father's words to her after marking the spots where her brothers should plant the hackmatacks.

"They're as good as money, Zena," he'd said. "Ask any shipbuilder in Scotty. He'll use the trunk and part of the root for the knees of the schooners. There's a natural bend there for supporting structures that come together at an angle, like the framing and deck beams. So if you're ever up against it in later years when I'm not here to help you...."

"Joe," she'd said, poking him in the ribs, "are you awake, Joe? I've thought of a way to help May."

At first light, he got out the pung, and they'd started toward Scotty, pulled over icy roads by their sharp shod horse, Ben. When they knocked at the door of a shipyard owner's house, his little curly haired boy, came to peek out at them. "Mama! Papa!" he shouted as he ran back toward the rear of the house. "It's the herb doctor!"

The shipyard owner, a big bear of a man, met Zena and Joe at the door with a welcoming smile, and ushered them into the fancy parlor with the Boston ferns and tied back velvet draperies. His tiny wife, came hurrying into the parlor a few minutes later, pinning a stray lock of hair into place. "Oh Mrs. Brown," she said, giving Zena a hug and a kiss, "it's so good to see you."

The hired girl served breakfast dainties—chopped ham in between two biscuits, baked one on top of another. She also brought cups of hot cocoa. The men had several helpings. Zena, a spartan eater, picked at the food placed on the parlor table beside her chair. When the hired girl had cleared away the dishes, the shipyard owner ceremoniously got out his box of expensive cigars from the drawer of his side table. Zena read the words, "The Bride of Key West" on the lid. He let Joe choose one, then took one for himself. "But for your good wife, mine wouldn't be here now," he said as he closed the box, "or the boy either. Stuck right with them, she did—day and night."

Joe told the shipyard owner about their daughter's need for money and asked if he'd buy the tall hackmatacks.

"I tell you what I'll do," he said heartily. "I'll pay in advance. Get the checkbook, dear."

"Mighty obliged," Joe said as he took the check.

"Glad to help."

When Zena and Joe were getting ready to leave, and Joe was talking to the shipyard owner, as the wife kissed Zena goodbye, she whispered "If I ever got sick, or in some way needed you very badly, would you come?"

"Of course I would, dear."

"Promise?"

"I promise."

The big man walked out to the buggy with them. The little boy, in a heavy coat, corduroy leggings and high boots, ran along beside them. Joe took the blanket off the horse, the hired girl placed towel wrapped re-heated bricks on the floor of the buggy, and the child began making a snowman.

Smiling jovially, the shipyard owner stepped over to where Joe stood, and held out two more cigars.

"Many thanks," Joe said.

She and Joe had driven from there to the bank to put the money in his small account, and before they left town, he'd mailed a check to East

Boston. On the way home, he had contentedly smoked one of the cigars that the shipyard owner had given him. "Good fellow, helping us out like that."

"Yes," Zena said, but a shadow of worry had stayed with her. She thought the young wife was pregnant, and she didn't know that she could get her through another birth.

Zena turned to look at Josie, who was singing the words to a new song: *"By the sea, by the sea, by the beautiful sea..."* as she pulled open the bottom drawer of the sideboard and lifted out a mulberry colored wool jacket.

The girl slipped into her new creation. "Look, Mother. Don't you think this turned out well? Do you think Lemmie will be pleased when I wear it to his wedding? Would anyone guess it was dyed and made over?"

"Of course Lemmie will be pleased. It looks perfect, and the material brand new." Josie has a special talent when it comes to fashion, Zena thought. When she walks downstreet in Scotty, even the well-off wives of master mariners turn to stare at her outfits.

"I'll make a hat, too," Josie said. She squinted her eyes, tried to picture what it should look like, then hurried over to the shelf behind the door to get the new December issue of *McCall's*, tripping over the brass spittoon in her haste. "Hattie Belle always likes the ones I make."

"I remember," Zena said. Everyone in the family knew the young woman well. Four years ago, when she'd taught at the one-room school down the road, she'd boarded at their house for three months.

"You'll laugh at this, Mother," Josie said, as she thumbed through the magazine. "When Frank came home that spring, I thought he was falling in love with her. I saw the way he winked at her across the supper table, and the way his hand touched hers when he passed the biscuits. I know now it was just a flirtation. Wasn't I a romantic child?"

"Most little girls are," Zena said. She turned abruptly to look out the window...where the hackmatacks used to be.

Her brother Frank's telegram had come just a few days after they'd sent the needed hackmatack money. She'd been sitting by the window braiding a little rug out of old stockings. As the grandfather clock struck four times, she heard a horse come into the yard. Turning her head, she'd seen the postmaster dismount. He carried a telegram, and as their eyes met, she knew it was bad news. It said, "May sick. Come now. Frank."

She'd used some of the remaining money from the sale of the trees to buy a train ticket to Boston. Frank had met her at North Station, and driven her to his house near Chelsea Creek. She'd held close the feverish child, who whispered, "I waited for you, Mother," and died in her arms. With the rest of the money, Zena had bought a casket to bring May's body home.

Zena couldn't let herself keep thinking about it. She had to get out of the house—out of that chair. "I think I'll go for the mail, Josie," she said. She took her bonnet and long black cloak from a row of nails by the kitchen door.

"You haven't eaten a thing, Mother, and it's almost noon."

Zena took a swallow of tea. "I'll eat when I get back." She started down the dirt road, which years before had been cut through a forest of pine and spruce. The tiny post office was only half a mile away. Beyond it stood their small white church; farther yet, the one room schoolhouse, which all the children had attended; then, on the opposite side of the road, the cemetery, where the family's tall white monument stood. The Masonic emblem at the top, with the big "G," for God in its center, sometimes gave her a measure of comfort. They'd recently paid for their daughter's epitaph to be chiseled onto the right hand side of the stone: "We loved her on earth, may we meet her in heaven."

She heard a sudden rustling in the undergrowth, and conscious of being completely alone, glanced about at the deep woods on either side. To her relief, a fox crossed the road a few yards in front of her. Panthers didn't come out till dark.

Zena turned into the area where the little post office stood, far back from the road. "Nothing today but the paper," the postmaster said as he pushed it out to her beneath the grate.

"It's all I expected. Letters from Percy and Lawrence came yesterday."

They were the only people in the post office, so she decided to visit for awhile, asking him about his loved ones, and telling him about her two boys at sea in their schooners and the one on his way home from Cuba and the Spanish War. As she came down the post office steps carrying her newspaper, she noticed that the air had grown close and heavy, and everything had become perfectly still. No wind moved the branches of the trees; no seagulls soared and screamed.

When her dark eyes looked up through the tree tops, she saw a strange bronze light, and knew the great storm was on its way. Fear for Percy and Lawrence, at sea in their schooners, clutched at her heart. Walking fast, Zena reached the clearing where her farmhouse stood atop Wawenock Ridge, banked with fir brush against the winter cold; and the weathered barn, to its far left, sat on a foundation of field stones. She hurried up the rise of the front yard. No sounds broke the stillness. The storm was going to be a heavy one and the animals sensed it.

Zena reached the top of the ridge, and gasping for breath, walked up three uneven slabs of granite and lifted the latch. The kitchen door swung open. A blend of aromas came out to meet her: beans baking in the oven, seasoned with molasses and salt pork; and of wood burning in the brick fireplace.

She stepped inside. Usually she felt a great pleasure in the sturdy little house with a fireplace in every room, but now she pictured Percy and Lawrence in an evil storm, as waves foamed across the deck, hatch covers blew off, and balls of blue light, St. Elmo's fire, danced mockingly at the tops of masts. She sighed heavily as she hung her cloak and bonnet on nails behind the door.

Josie, who had fallen asleep at the treadle sewing machine, lifted her head and pushed thick auburn hair away from her face. The mulberry colored wool skirt lay in her lap.

"Look outside, child," Zena said.

As Josie stood up and rubbed her eyes, her long hair fell over her pleated sleeves and down her back. She tucked her shirtwaist into her floor length black skirt as she walked.

A few feet before she reached the window, she came to an abrupt stop, then began running toward it. "That strange light! A heavy gale's coming!"

Chapter 3

Be Careful Tonight, My Children

"Pray for the boys, Josie."

"I am, Mother."

"Your father's in the barn?" Zena asked.

"Not home yet."

"Not home yet? I can't believe it." Zena paced up and down in front of the window, then stopped to stare down Wawenock Ridge to the road. She tapped her long fingers on the window sash, willing her husband Joe, in his heavy coat and old fedora with the turned down brim, to ride out from between the trees that lined the road on either side. No sign of him. "Your father took his gun?"

"No."

The grandfather clock struck three times. Joe needed to get home soon. It would start getting dark at four. After sunset the panther might return. "We'll do the chores now," she said. "You fork down the hay. I'll start milking. I'll take orts to the hens. You fill the woodboxes."

Zena and Josie began changing from house clothes to patched and faded shirts, skirts, and jackets hanging on nails by the side door. Every couple of minutes they glanced through the window at the ominous bronze light.

As Zena reached for a shirt, she tried to figure out, from yesterday's letters, exactly where Lawrence and Percy would be when the storm hit. Lawrence's letter, dated November 20, had come from New York. He said the lime casks had been unloaded and the holds were to be filled with coal. Then he'd sail north to Salem, Massachusetts. He should be at sea by now—might be close to Cape Cod.

Zena stepped into an old wool skirt, buttoned the waist band, and tried to determine where Percy would be. His letter, also dated November 20, said he'd anchored the *Addie E.* off St. Helena Island in East Penobscot Bay.

She put on an old black bonnet, then tied the strings beneath her chin. Percy had written he was waiting for the schooner to be filled with paving stones. She sighed and stuck her long slender feet into sturdy shoes with scuffed toes. He said he wanted to head south for New York by the twenty fourth. Today was the twenty sixth. He might be near Cape Cod, too, but sailing in the opposite direction from Lawrence. Lemmie was safe, away from the coming storm.

Josie, now in the kitchen of the small house, paused in her ladling of warm water from stove well into a tin pail, and looked out again at the strange bronze light. "I wish Percy weren't carrying stone. Maybe he can ride out the storm in a safe harbor."

"Let's hope so." Zena set four seamless milk pails, made of extra heavy tin, just inside the door to keep them clean, and took with her only the light pail that had been filled with warm water for washing off the cows' udders.

"I'm going to run ahead," Josie said, "and start pitching down the hay." Within a few minutes, the cows in the barnyard heard the hay falling, and ambled through the door in single file, the boss cow leading the way. Zena, using her hands, washed down their udders with warm water. Smudge, the dark grey cat, jumped from the loft, and crouched on the lid of a barrel waiting for her saucer of milk. Her kittens were carefully hidden in a nest-like place in the hay.

Josie, who had begun at the far end of the barn, pitching hay down into feed boxes, was finished. "Eek!" she cried, just before she started down the ladder. "A mouse ran over my foot." The cat watched from the shadows, yellow eyes glowing.

"She'll get him before morning," Zena said.

Josie emptied the bucket of water onto the ground outside the barn door, and ran back to the house for the milk pails. When finished with the milking, they walked toward the house, each carrying two full pails. The bronze light had started to fade, and the wind began. "I'm afraid for Percy," Josie said as she put down her milk pails and opened the side door. "I wish things were the way they used to be, with Lawrence captain of the *Addie E.* and Percy mate. But now Lawrence is captain of the *Robert A.* and Percy is master of the old vessel. If only Percy didn't have to deal with this heavy storm all alone."

Zena held several thicknesses of cheese cloth, and knotted the ends together at either side of the pail above the milk. She knew she couldn't give in to fear or she couldn't keep steady when the storm came. "Percy's not alone, Josie," she said, as they began the job of straining the milk through cheesecloth into pans. "He has a good crew. They're all from around Rockland. Grew up on the water, the way our boys did."

As they put the milk pans on shelves in the cellarway, she added, "Percy has all his skills. Passed his written tests, too. Lawrence was so proud, he whittled him a model of the *Addie E.* for a gift."

"Yes. That was so sweet," Josie said. Her unusual mahogany colored eyes met Zena's piercing black ones. In that sentimental moment the only sounds in the house were made by the crackle of the fire on the hearth.

Josie took a deep breath. "They'll both be fine," she declared in a firm voice, as if making herself believe it. "They'll get back to Rockland, anchor behind the breakwater, and head home to Blueberry Farm."

The boys called the place by that name because each summer blueberries covered half the front yard, so thick that the very earth seemed blue. Zena prayed they would get home safely.

Exhausted from work and worry Zena quickly changed back into her house clothes, and sank down in the rocker by the window to watch for Joe. In bygone days, his mother, Prudence, had sat there so often, looking up the road toward Scotty for her husband and seafaring sons to come home, that his little sister had called it "the worry chair."

Josie went out again and returned with wood from a white birch that had fallen and been chopped up for firewood. "I'm going back for more," she said. "I'm going to pile the kitchen woodbox really high, the ones in the bedrooms, too."

"Good," Zena said, beginning work on a torn shirt. Every little while, she lifted her head to look out the window for her husband.

Josie, on her last trip, brought in a basketful of maple kindling, then changed into her house clothes and began straightening the kitchen. She closed the sewing machine, and carefully laid the new skirt in the long bottom drawer of the sideboard. She bent to pick up several dropped pins. "I hate it that Percy is carrying paving stones," she blurted out, in spite of her brave words of a few minutes ago. "Lemmie carried paving stones when he got shipwrecked on the *Sheepscot*."

Zena remembered all too well. When the schooner was caught in heavy seas, she rolled and pitched, and those paving stones shifted in the hold. The men couldn't pump water out of her fast enough. Finally the pumps broke. Now Percy was taking the same course and carrying the same cargo.

"But the *Addie E.* is a bigger vessel than the *Sheepscot*, isn't she?" Josie asked. "Wouldn't that make her safer?"

"I remember the *Sheepscot* as 86 feet long, and the *Addie E.* as 95. Does that make her safer? I don't know."

How Zena wished Percy had been content to stay on the farm. The spring after he'd graduated from the eighth grade, he had started helping his father. Like his brothers and classmates, he hadn't gone on to high school. One day, when they were planting potatoes not far from the house, she had pushed up the pantry window a crack to listen to what they were talking about, and heard the boy's merry laughter at one of Joe's stories. It had sounded good.

The next summer Captain Fitch, their neighbor and Joe's cousin, had asked Percy if he'd like to go along as cabin boy on a run to New

Orleans. The boy was delighted. He brought home a ship in a bottle and placed it on the mantel under the painting of his grandfather's favorite vessel, the *Barque Noble*, and next to her log. He bragged all winter about that port, and particularly about the food. "Those red snappers," he told everyone, "best fish I ever ate."

"Surely your father will come soon," Zena said. But, although they watched by the window, there was no sign of him. What if something had happened? She began to tap her foot nervously. Out of the corner of her eye, she saw her daughter looking at her with an anxious expression.

"Don't worry, Mother," Josie said. "Father will come along soon. The boys will make port, then we'll get their letters. We'll feel foolish for fretting."

"Maybe so."

Josie turned away from the window and walked over to stand in front of the kitchen looking glass. "My hair is a mess." She lifted some of her hair combings from a lidded china bowl, used them to fill in a soft pompadour, then pulled back the rest of her long hair and tied it with a wide lavender ribbon. She glanced at her mother. "I'm going to stop worrying. I really mean it!"

Zena knew Josie couldn't stop worrying, any more than she herself could. How thankful she'd be to have the storm over, and Percy, Lawrence and Myrtie Belle here, safe and sound. Like scenes from a play, she saw them seated around the table at mealtime, joking and laughing, then exchanging Christmas gifts in front of the hearth. The only person missing would be Lemmie.

When she was a young woman, still living at her parents' home, there had been a special Christmas, special because her father and all her brothers except one were home from sea at the same time.   Everyone had remarked on it. Not until a few weeks later had they learned his ship, while

The ADDIE E. SNOW

returning from the Caribbean, had gone down in a hurricane off Cape Fear, North Carolina. The great storm had come up from the Gulf of Mexico.

She thought of Lemmie's ship returning home from the Caribbean. Was he nearing Cape Fear, with its jutting sandbars? No, I won't let myself think it could happen again—and at Christmas time, she told herself sternly.   She struggled to put her mind on something pleasant—his upcoming marriage to Hattie Belle—and picture all of them dressed in wedding finery, at her father's big home on Pemaquid Bay. But her mind was caught in a maze of worry.

Mending a tear in Joe's shirt, Zena noticed missing buttons. She hunted in her button jar, then re-threaded her needle. She wished that when Percy had become a captain, he'd been given a vessel other than the *Addie E.* Some people called her a bad luck schooner. The boys had said it really had nothing to do with her safety; it was because a captain, who'd been master of her before Lawrence, just happened to get a bad crew. Still, she would have felt easier if, as a new captain, Percy had been given a different vessel.

"Stop worrying, Mother," Josie said. "Let's think about something happy. Remember a couple of weeks after Lawrence and Myrtie Belle's wedding, how they and Percy dropped by for a visit?"

Lawrence had anchored the *Addie E. Snow* in the Damariscotta River, they'd rowed ashore, then walked up the lane at the far edge of woods and fields. When Zena had glanced out the pantry window, to pleasure her eyes at the view she loved, she spied them talking and laughing as they came past the hen house toward the side door. Lawrence was carrying Myrtie Belle's banjo.

Zena's heart had leaped with joy at the sight of them, and at the same time she'd thought of Lemmie, Lawrence's twin, they were so exactly alike. Two years ago she had looked out the same window and seen him, dressed in foreign clothes, and looking worn and thin, come walking up through the fields toward the house.

Not long after Percy, Lawrence, and Myrtie Belle had come inside, the bride, in an old rose silk shirtwaist and silver grey skirt, played the banjo and sang the new song, "By the Sea." As she sang, Lawrence's eyes had never left her face. When she'd finished, and he'd told a funny story, she'd giggled, "Oh, you are so clever, Lonnie!"—her pet name for him. When his tales became more and more hilarious, the 17-year-old bride's carefree laughter had rung like silver bells through the old farmhouse. Then she had run across the room, jumped into his lap, and kissed him.

Oh, let Lawrence hurry to port and wait out the storm, Zena prayed.

She knew from experience that if Lawrence were shipwrecked, or if Lemmie, the other twin would be shipwrecked within the next few days. They were so alike they were almost the same person. The summer they were eleven, Lawrence, as he sailed back from the grocery store at Poole's Landing in Edgecomb, overturned their homemade boat and lost everything. Lemmie did the same thing the next week.

A few days after Lemmie had been shipwrecked, in '96, Lawrence had been also. Whatever happened to one of the twins, happened to the other. Although she had never given voice to her fears, she believed if one of them were lost at sea, the other would be too.

"It will be great to have Percy, Lawrence and Myrtie Belle home in a couple of weeks," Josie said. "We'll have an early Christmas. I wish Lemmie could be here, too. Our celebration won't be the same without him."

"Yes," Zena said, "having him home would be wonderful, but he is on his way." The family had a lot to be thankful for. Not all the boys who fought in the Spanish War would be coming home. She and Joe had worried Lemmie might be killed in the fighting, but it was malaria that nearly did him in. The newspapers reported less than 400 boys killed in battle, while some 5,000 had died from illness.

She knew one of the things Joe wanted to do in Scotty was to get a supply of quinine, or Peruvian Bark, as some called it, to have on hand for Lemmie when he came home from Cuba. Although recovered from malaria, he would still need the tonic from time to time. A person was never completely cured. When the spells came, the skin and even the white of the eyes took on a yellow hue.

Every few minutes she paused in her mending to glance out the window. Where could Joe be? The errands shouldn't take this long. Had he stopped to visit his cousin Elmer Fitch, a steam fitter for the big ships, or to spend a little time with one of his elderly aunts? Several of the houses up the road were owned by Fitches, his mother's people.

Most likely, Joe and Simon had stayed too long at the livery stable listening to gossip and swapping tall tales. She wished he would hurry. Once a storm began, any number of things could happen on the five miles of rough roads running between Scotty and Walpole. Often a loud crash of thunder or streak of lightening had caused a horse to bolt, tipping over a buggy and throwing out the riders.

The thought flashed into her mind that Joe might be at a friend's who lived near Scotty. Some of the local men went there for drinks of home brew. But she discarded the idea. He knew how she felt about strong drink, except for medicinal purposes, of course.

The Grandfather Clock in the little front hall struck four times. When she looked outside again, it was into the day's fading light. "It's starting to get dark, Josie," she said.

"I'm sure father will be here soon. At least he is on dry land. Do you think Lemmie is really on his way home from Cuba now? First he thought he was coming in late August, then September, then October...."

"I believe he really is now. In his last letter he said the *Scorpion* should be at sea before Thanksgiving, making passage for New York."

"Next year I'll be away from home," Josie said—"in Boston. I'm going to work hard at my tailoring and millinery classes. You're going to be so proud."

Zena, who had known too much sadness to come from Boston, wondered if she could let the child go.

"Won't it be fun to go to Lemmie's wedding," Josie said. "I'm glad it will be in Pemaquid Harbor instead of a far-away place like Rockland. Do you think he will be married in his dress uniform? That would make the ceremony very elegant."

Zena held up her long hands in protest. "Land sakes, child, I don't care about that. All I care about is Lemmie getting home safe and sound. I tell you, Josie, some nights during the war I prayed so hard I could feel the virtue being drawn out of me, and come morning I was most too tired to get up."

When her brothers, Eph and Frank, were in the War of the Rebellion, her mother's lips had moved in constant prayer as she'd rolled out the biscuits, spun the wool, churned the butter....

Both boys had returned home, but in vastly different conditions. Eph had come back from Company I of the 21st regiment of Maine Volunteers weak and frail, just out of the hospital, and only partially recovered from a combination of typhoid fever and measles. But when Frank had come home unscathed from Company D of the 14th regiment of Maine Volunteers, sporting a full beard, walking with a cocky swagger, and telling war stories, he was a village hero.

She wished Frank hadn't come into her mind. Joe and I should never have trusted him and his wife to take care of our daughter, she told herself again. If he'd let me know sooner that she was ill, the old Abenaki ways might have saved her.

Zena strained to look through the long row of leafless lilac bushes that bordered the yard, so she might see up the road to where the trees began. If only Joe would hurry. With a sigh, she turned away from the window, and caught sight of her reflection in the kitchen looking glass. As she walked toward it, she tried to push in place a stray lock of her straight black hair. "I'll have to let it down and start over," she said. "That old bonnet pulled it all adrift."

Josie, moving as gracefully as a dancer, began taking the dishes from the shelf. With her beautiful hair, and pretty features, she might have stepped out of the pages of her *McCall's* magazine. She laid the white ironstone dishes, napkin rings and tin knives, forks and spoons in precise patterns on the red oilcloth.

Zena parted her long black hair in the middle and pulled it back. The looking glass reflected flawless copper toned skin, high cheek bones, and piercing dark eyes—her mother's face. She finished with her hair in just a few minutes, yet still stood in front of the old looking glass with its heavy cherry wood frame. Wondering where the boys might be when the storm came, she absently ran a long forefinger across a crack at the top of the glass. It had once been aboard one of Joe's father's ships. A broken one was bad luck, and the captain wouldn't take it to sea again.

Perhaps bad luck was the family fate. A feeling of foreboding enveloped her as she thought of Joe's father, lost in the December gale of 1856, on his way to Africa in the *Barque Estella*. His father before him had been lost in an ice storm while rounding Cape Horn.

Then the face of her oldest son, Frank, auburn haired and handsome, appeared in her mind's eye. He had been lost on the schooner *Mavooshen* in the February storm of 1895, his vessel loaded with coal from Philadelphia.

Be careful tonight, my children, be careful, she silently willed those at sea. Sail for the nearest port and stay till the storm is over.

I don't think I could survive the loss of another child.

Chapter 4

The Village of Pemaquid Harbor

Hattie Belle

Hattie Belle Davis, in a fashionable black cape with bear fur trim, walked slowly down the long sloping yard toward the shore. She crossed the rutted lane, opened the gate in the stone wall and started down the path. In bad times she had gone, even as a child, to sit on the rocks and listen to the comforting sound of water lapping against them.

Her blue-grey eyes, underlined with dark half-circles, looked out over the harbor, where brightly painted lobstermen's buoys bobbed in dark blue water. Shortly after midnight, a horrible dream about Lemmie's ship, the *Scorpion*, had caused her to lay awake until daybreak.

Waves of depression swept over Hattie Belle as she thought of her situation — her mercurial stepmother, one moment kind, the next cruel; and the frustration of a long delayed wedding. She'd waited for two and a half years, through shipwreck, debt repayment and war.

In August Lemmie had written from Cuba:

"Get that wedding gown out of mothballs, Love. The war is over and we're coming home. Don't sign up to teach. Being my wife is going to take all your time."

The fleet did come home, but the *Scorpion* was given what he called "wipe-up" duty.

"You won't believe this, Love. We're staying on to take army engineers to find stable places for building wharves. Why? So our transports can load the captives and take them back to Spain. Everyone on board this ship is fed up. We won the war but the losers get to go home."

Not until his letter written the first week of November, did he have

good news.

"The *Scorpion* has orders to sail for New York. Our replacement ship arrives next week. We should be on our way before Thanksgiving, Love.

Can't wait, Love."

Hattie Belle had danced around her bedroom. She'd been happy and light-hearted for the past two weeks. So after a row of pleasant dreams of Lemmie and the wedding, why this evil nightmare of the *Scorpion* caught in the trough of the sea? She needed time to herself to sort things out—to decide if this were just a meaningless dream or a sign that Lemmie wouldn't be coming home—ever.

Her father and stepmother's trip to Damariscotta, the last before winter set in, provided the opportunity to be alone. Even the lobstermen in their dories were far from shore.

Sitting on a large rock above a beach of rough sand covered with broken shells, she breathed in the salt air, and listened to wavelets lap against the shore. Seagulls gave their mournful cries, dove for fish, and were beautiful in flight. The sky was clear except for a few clouds along the horizon.

Directly across the harbor, at Pemaquid Beach, a sturdy three-masted schooner, the *Henry H. Chamberlain*, tugged gently at her moorings. To the south Hattie Belle saw the ruins of four old forts, then Witch Island, Christmas Cove Point, and the expanse of John's Bay running into the ocean. She turned to look north, up river toward Pemaquid Falls, past an artificial mound on the top of a hill, a fortification built by people who'd lived there long ago, and where she had played as a child. The familiar sights, sounds and smells brought some comfort.

Too soon, however, her hands and feet began to ache with the cold as a freezing wind blew along the water. Starting back up the path, she looked beyond the stone wall, to the big white house looming at the top of the hill. Once it had been a home filled with laughter and music.

While removing her fur trimmed cape, a strand of light brown hair flecked with gold worked loose from tortoise shell hairpins. With cold-stiffened fingers Hattie Belle tucked it into the pretty roll at the nape of her neck. She collected the breakfast dishes, washed and dried them. Next she drained the water from the yellow eye beans which had been soaking overnight, put in fresh water, and heated them slowly until the skins burst, drained the beans again and prepared them for baking, burying a rind of salt pork in them, and pouring over them a mix of molasses, salt and sugar, then boiling water. They'd have to bake all day to be ready for supper. When the beans were in the oven, she filled the woodbox, then swept the floor.

Tired from worry and lack of sleep, Hattie Belle lay down for a cat nap on the living room couch. On awakening, several hours later, her mood had lifted. A dream, no matter how real it seemed, had yet to be proven. As she prepared the brown bread from Indian meal, graham flour, soda, salt, molasses and sour milk, she decided to act as if Lemmie's return were a certainty and he would soon be sailing into New York Harbor.

After turning the well mixed ingredients into a one pound coffee can, tying the lid down with a string, and setting the mold on a trivet in boiling water, Hattie Belle took her box of writing materials from the sideboard and seated herself in one of the captain's chairs that lined the kitchen table. Dipping her steel pointed pen into a bottle of blue ink, she began writing in a clear Spencerian hand, "Dearest Lemmie," and finished pages later with, "Love always."

Hattie Belle stuck the letter into an envelope, then picked up a stick of pink, perfumed sealing wax. She lit the wick with a wooden match, dropped molten wax on the envelope's closed flap, and pressed a metal seal with the initial "H" into the soft circle. Holding it there for a moment, she heard the slow rhythm of Old John's hooves echoing from the road at the back of the house.

Hattie Belle was putting her writing materials back into the box when Captain Davis, a sturdy man with greying mutton chop whiskers and steel blue eyes, strode into the kitchen, his arms full of purchases. She turned in her chair. "You're home early, Papa."

"Ayuh," he said as he laid the packages on the table: a roll of blue and white checked gingham for making aprons, a one pound box of Arm and Hammer saleratus for getting biscuits to rise; a bottle of Lydia Pinkham, a vegetable compound for helping middle aged women feel spry; a fancy porcelain chamber pot decorated with pink azaleas; and a case of Bull Durham smoking tobacco.

"I've written a letter to Lemmie, Papa. He'll find it waiting when he sails into New York."

"Good idea."

If through the grace of God he gets there, Hattie Belle silently added, remembering last night's terrible dream, in spite of herself.

"Left earlier than we'd planned," Captain Davis said. "Heavy weather's coming."

"Heavy weather? When I went outside a while ago, the sky was bright blue. Hardly a cloud."

"Red flags are up in Scotty," he said. "Telegrams came to the shipping companies. Straight from Washington. Heavy weather's on the way."

Hattie Belle's eyes registered concern.

Crossing the kitchen in his rolling sea walk, the captain took the barometer off its hook and held it up. "Just as I thought. The mercury is dropping like a stone through water."

When he stood beside her chair to show her the instrument, the salt water and tar smell of his old pea jacket, kept for years in his sea chest, carried her back in an instant to her childhood. She remembered him coming through the doorway of their house in Long Cove, just home from sea. He had picked her up and swung her high in the air, hugged her half-sister May, then walked with his arm about Mama to look at the new baby asleep in his cradle near the kitchen stove. "He's a mighty handsome boy, Gussie," her father said.

The house owned by Capt. Davis, where Hattie Belle grew up
Pemaquid Harbor

He had been slender then, with no grey in his thick sandy hair or his mutton chop whiskers, and his light blue eyes were full of laughter.

"I named him Elmer," Mama said, "after our first little boy." And Hattie Belle had seen the look of sorrow that passed between them.

Why does sorrow so often lurk at the edge of happiness? she asked herself. Are sad memories "the little foxes" the Bible speaks of, "the little foxes that spoil the vines?"

Captain Davis stood looking out one of the big nine over six kitchen windows, his back to the table where his daughter sat. "We were almost home when your mother saw a friend of hers going into the post office. She insisted on getting out of the buggy. Said she would walk home. I don't like the idea, Mary, I told her. You could get caught in sleet and heavy winds. But that didn't stop her. The woman's inclined to be strong minded."

That's an understatement, Hattie Belle thought, but aloud she said, "It's not but five hundred yards. She'll be all right."

"Ayuh. I expect. But when it does come, it'll be a Hell-Ripper. That bronze sky—it's bad news."

"Bronze sky?" She got up from her chair so fast it would have tipped over if she hadn't caught it by the back. She ran to a window. "Oh my! Why didn't you tell me? I've been sitting here, writing, facing the wall. It looks dreadful outside! Dreadful!"

"Puts me in mind of another time there was this kind of light in the sky and this kind of dead feeling in the air," Captain Davis said. "We were in the West Indies. Went there with a cargo of box shooks and barrel staves. Traded for coffee, rum and muscovado."

He paused to take off his pea coat and his corduroy cap with the ear flaps. "By gorry, when the hurricane struck, we weren't but a day out of Matanzas, Cuba. A one hundred mile wind whirled my schooner like a top. Tons of foaming sea washed over her. She lost her deck load and bowsprit. Those hogsheads of raw sugar—they weigh half a ton apiece—broke loose in the hold and...."

"Listen, Papa, listen," she interrupted. "Lemmie expected the *Scorpion* to leave Cuba before Thanksgiving. I don't know how many days ago she left. But I think she may have been caught in the beginnings of this storm. If we find the gale is coming from the south—I think there's a good chance it began in the Gulf of Mexico and overtook the ship in the South Atlantic." She paused to take a deep breath.

Captain Davis looked puzzled. "Why makes you say that?"

*Capt. William Davis
when young*

"I had a dreadful dream. I saw the *Scorpion* rolling and pitching. A heavy cross sea struck, breaking the wheel. Like a flash the ship fell off into the trough, and the sea washed over her. Out of the spray and foam I saw Lemmie and another fellow making their way aft. Lemmie carried halyards snatched from the flagstaff...used them to lash jacking bars to the wheel.

"I woke up with a jolt, Papa, wringing wet and trembling. I don't know what I'll do if I've lost Lemmie."

"If he got that wheel mended in a hurry, and I know how quick Lem is, the bow could have come right up from that hollow between the waves. The ship would be saved."

"Do you really think so, Papa?"

"It's a good possibility," he said, then reached out a work-roughened hand and patted her on the shoulder.

Hattie Belle nodded, acknowledging his concern, then turned away from the window. "I want to stand on the piazza now...see from which way the heavy weather's coming."

She took her knitted blue shawl from the back of her chair and walked from the kitchen, through the living-dining room with its big fireplace, where before the days of the cookstove Grandmother Lewis had stirred the clam chowder, baked the beans, and steamed the brown bread. In the hall, she pulled open the front door and stepped out onto the piazza.

In the bronze haze, the well-loved scene before her, from the trees next to the house, to the rutted lane at the bottom of the big yard her took on a strange, even unreal appearance. Even the stone wall on the far side of the lane, and the path that led from its gate, down to the landing where the water lapped against the rocky shore, seemed somehow unfamiliar.

Her nightmare had now become a firm reality in her mind. She visualized the gunboat, with the broken steering wheel, caught in the trough of the sea, great waves sweeping over the deck. Was it possible the vessel could survive?

There was nothing to do but wait and pray. As a sea captain's daughter, she knew this agony well. She remembered as a very little girl, her mother and half-sister May keeping vigil for her father through many a dreadful storm. Living as they did, on a mile long peninsula at the edge of the North Atlantic, they felt the violent lashings of line gales, and understood some of the terror of those at sea.

When Hattie Belle grew old enough to seriously consider marriage, she remembered the look of suffering in her mother's eyes during the storms, and resolved not to wed a mariner. But ninety percent of the young men went to sea. On that rocky land with the thin acidic soil there were few other ways to make a decent living.

In February of '96, Hattie Belle had resisted Captain Lemuel Brown's courtship through weekly letters. Her short return messages, written for the sake of politeness, were quite formal. The box of chocolate creams and folio of favorite songs were ignored. It had been little more than a year since losing her "first love," and she'd promised herself not to fall in love with another seafaring man. The pain outweighed the happiness.

But when in early March Captain Lemuel Brown had come calling at her boarding house in Pemaquid Point, she'd felt herself weakening. Even now, more than two and a half years later, she remembered exactly the way he looked as he came through the parlor doorway in his navy blue suit and matching overcoat, and carrying his bowler hat. How could she resist the black curly hair and sweeping moustache, the twinkle in his eye, the cleft in his chin, and the bronzed skin from his years at sea? Was it fair that he was so handsome? Her foolish heart broke the promise.

He wrote from Green's Landing on Deer Isle, saying he planned to leave April first, bound for New York and carrying granite paving stones. She was thinking of him that cold Wednesday morning as she wrote on the blackboard the week's memory verse. It was the third stanza of his favorite poem, *The Wreck of the Hesperus*.

> "The Skipper he stood beside the helm,
> His pipe was in his mouth
> And he watched how the veering flaw did blow
> The smoke now West, now South."

She pictured Lemmie in his heavy clothes and high boots, clay pipe in his mouth, steering the heavily laden schooner *Sheepscot* between the spruce covered islands in East Penobscot Bay.

He had promised to send a letter from Portland. She should have heard in a day or two, but a week had gone by. During that stormy week, she would awaken off and on through the night, imagining his schooner in all kinds of trouble. Something had to be wrong. The pain of loving a seafaring man had begun.

Standing on the piazza, Hattie Belle shivered in the cold, damp air, and hugged the shawl tightly about herself. She heard the creak of an opening door, and turned to see her father standing behind her.

In his left hand he carried his old brass spy-glass with a hand-grip of brown leather stretched tightly around it. In his right hand he held her black cape with the bear fur trim, which he gently adjusted on her delicate shoulders. "Don't want you getting chilled."

It was now late afternoon, and the lobstermen, in their yellow oilskins, were working their way toward shore in their dories, every now and then glancing up at the strangely colored sky. Captain Davis, standing at the edge of the piazza, his spyglass in tucked under one arm, cupped his hands at either side of his mouth, shouted "Ahoy there!" then waved. Two of the men closest to shore heard and waved back.

He clapped his telescope to his right eye. Hattie Belle, standing at his side, followed the direction of his searching gaze. From their high point overlooking the inner harbor of the Pemaquid River, they looked east above the area where the lobstermen were, then on toward Pemaquid Beach, the village directly across the harbor.

Capt. Lemuel Brown

"*Chamberlain's* sitting low in the water," Captain Davis said. "It's no wonder. She's carrying all the machinery that tried the oil out of the Porgies. Hundreds of barrels of the oil, too. Hate to see the factory gone. That Porgy oil can't be beat for mixing with paint or dressing leather."

Hattie Belle hated the way it made paint smell. Her room, above the boarding house parlor where Lemmie visited, had been dreary, so with her landlady's consent, she'd begun painting it with a can of left-over Prussian blue from home.

She remembered how unpleasantly strong the smell had been at night, as she lay in the darkness, listening to the waves crash against the rocks and to the endless ringing of the fog bell. Where could Lemmie be? Was he still alive?

The physical act of painting afforded some relief from sitting in her room correcting papers, or staring out the small window at the faded red barn. She remembered coming home from school one afternoon with the intention of painting the last remaining wall. Intending to change out of her good blue broadcloth shirtwaist and floor length grey skirt, she was unbuttoning the cuff on a leg o'mutton sleeve when she heard the landlady coming up the back stairway from the kitchen.

"Yoo hoo! Miss Davis!" she called. As Hattie Belle opened her door, she saw the thin frizzy haired woman gain the top step and start down the hall, carrying a newspaper in one of her chapped red hands. "I'm afraid I have some worrisome news about your young man. Here in today's paper is a piece about the *Sheepscot*." She pointed to the Shipping News.

"N.Y., April 10th, The Str. Trinidad from Bermuda reports having passed sch. Sheepscot on fire 180 miles southeast of Sandy Hook."

On fire at sea...what could be worse? Hattie Belle, feeling suddenly weak and dizzy, had sunk down onto the bed.

"Lie back on the pillow," the landlady said. She unbuttoned Hattie Belle's needle toe kid shoes, took them off, and lifted her stockinged feet onto the bed. She dipped Hattie Belle's washcloth into the big blue and white water pitcher, wrung it out, and laid it on her forehead. "Don't give up, Miss Davis. My husband says you should write to the captain of the *Trinidad*—send it in care of the newspaper."

Before long, Hattie Belle was at her writing desk, begging the captain for any further information he might give her.

Several afternoons later, the landlady came rushing up the back stairway again, this time with a later copy of the newspaper. "Good news, Miss Davis," she cried. "Here's what we've been waiting for," and she read aloud: "The reply of Captain Wasen of the *Trinidad* to inquiries about the *Sheepscot*: 'I passed sch. Sheepscot April 9th at 4 p.m., 180 miles south east of Sandy Hook on fire in the cabin. A steamer bound east had been along-side shortly before I got along-side and had taken off the crew.'"

Hattie Belle gave the landlady at hug. "Thank you. Wonderful news!" For the first time in what seemed like months, she was able to sleep soundly through the night. Two days later the Shipping News had more information about Lemmie's schooner.

"A Captain Aiken, spoke the British steamer *County of York*, from Philadelphia to Libau. She had on board the crew of the American schr. *Sheepscot*, which had been abandoned at sea."

It had been an unexpected treat to know what ship Lemmie was on and where he was headed. She'd found Libau on her world map. The old Latvian port, now a part of Russia, had seemed a long way from home.

While Captain Davis studied the big three master across the harbor, Hattie Belle concentrated on the building that housed the dance hall. On several moonlit evenings when Lemmie was home from sea, they'd rowed there, and waltzed the night away.

She and her father looked south along that eastern shore, above the ruins of the four old forts. She and Lemmie had walked there, arm in arm, along the ancient streets. He'd stopped to look at a great rock with the date 1607 carved in it. "That's thirteen years before the Pilgrims came to Plymouth," he'd commented.

"No signs yet of which way the heavy gales are coming," Captain Davis said. Suddenly he turned his head back to look directly across the river again, drawn by his intense interest in the big sea-going vessel.

Hattie Belle sighed, and remembered the local saying about retired mariners: "The salt never gets out of their blood."

"I've heard Captain Fossett has left two men on the *Chamberlain* to stand guard," Captain Davis said. "The rest of the crew will board in the morning. Except for drinking water and food stores, they must be ready to sail. Sure hate to see that porgy factory gone. But now those fish don't come farther north than Cape Cod."

He walked down the two steps and out into the front yard. "Don't see your mother coming. Hope she gets home soon." Frowning, he returned to the piazza, opened the front door a crack and shouted, "You home yet, Mary?" No answer. Captain Davis again put his spyglass to his eye and turned to look north, up river past the mysterious fort now covered with bushes. To Hattie Belle's inquiring, "Papa?" he shook his head. Her mother's brother, Uncle George Lewis, and his friend, Captain Lorenzo McLain, used to do a lot of digging around there. They'd found cannon balls bigger than those at the forts across the river and a long curved knife called a machete. When the war with Spain broke out, she'd shuddered as she read that some of the natives used them to fight with.

"Believe I'll go down near the stone wall and take a good look around," he said.

Hattie Belle felt sure that as yet no dark clouds had appeared from any direction. She looked down toward the stone wall, and relived a special spring Sunday, when she'd gone to sit there and look out over the water, relax, and enjoy nature's beauty.

It was the last Sunday in May of '96. That morning she'd gone to church at Pemaquid Falls with her father and stepmother. After the service, they'd been invited by friends to Sunday dinner. She could have gone, too, but said she really needed to rest a bit before returning to her boarding house. Weariness had set in from Saturday's scrubbing of the bath house, then the washing and ironing of table and bed linens—all in preparation for the summer boarders.

As they were leaving church, a neighbor, who lived farther down Pemaquid Harbor Road, offered her a ride home.

Not wanting to bother with making a meal, Hattie Belle poured herself a cup of tea from the pot at the back of the stove, and picked up a couple of molasses cookies. While she nibbled on a cookie and took sips of tea, she watched the water and enjoyed the sun, the salt air, and the cries of the birds.

Because of the screams of the circling gulls, and the cawing of the crows, she didn't hear the horse's hooves on the road that to the barn at the back of the house. The first she knew anyone was behind her was when a hand with an anchor and shield tattoo covered hers. She was so startled she almost fell.

"Hattie," he said, "get down off that stone wall and give me a kiss." And dropping the cookies and spilling the tea, in her haste, she did.

After awhile he reached into his pocket and took out a small silver box with a dome of gold plush. Opening it with shaking hands, Hattie Belle found inside a gold ring with a row of four rubies. "Oh Lemmie! It's beautiful!" she exclaimed, laughing and crying at the same time.

"Bought the ring in Russia," he said. "When the crew and I were leaving the *County of York* Captain Maddrell gave us each a gold piece. Felt sorry for us, I guess. We were a pitiful sight...ragged clothes, and boots tied on with cordline. Anyhow, with what he gave us and the money I had in my pocket, I had enough to buy it."

"Boots tied on with cordline?"

"We'd been on our feet day and night through a week of storms. I stood at the wheel. Had to keep her out of the trough. Water rushed in through the seams, so everyone else kept bailing. Our feet got swollen so bad our boots had to be cut off."

She pressed her lips tightly together to keep from crying.

"I've lost all the things a captain depends on," he said, "my charts, and my instruments: chronometer, sextant, compass.... Also lost the pay I'd get after delivering the stone to New York. Right now this ring is all I have to offer. Do I dare ask the prettiest girl in Lincoln County to wait for me?"

"Oh yes, Lemmie," she'd breathed. "Oh yes!"

Chapter 5

Hard-a-lee

Hattie Belle

Captain Davis searched the sky above the house, then lowered the spyglass and shook his head. On his return up the rise of the front yard, he looked toward the road which led to the back of the house, and came to a stop. "There's your mother coming now. About time she got here."

"Oh dear!" Hattie Belle said under her breath. "Neither the tea nor the coffee is made, and the table isn't set."

She threw open the front door, ran through the house, and into the kitchen. Quickly lifting the hinged lid of the black enameled coffee canister, she tossed a handful of the ground beans into the aluminum coffeepot, then setting it in the black iron sink, pumped in cold well-water. She scooped tea leaves from a matching canister into the long-spouted teapot, then poured in water from the kettle at the back of the woodstove and set it over the water tank on the right side of the stove to steep. To hurry the coffee along, she opened the draft on the left side and stirred the fire with all her strength.

She heard the side door in the back hall open, and from around the corner, heard her stepmother call her name.

"Hattie Belle?"

"Yes, Mother."

"Did you get the beans started early enough this morning—or did you just sit around—the way you like to do?"

Hattie Belle didn't answer. Once, when she was fifteen, she hadn't started the beans in time for them to bake the necessary eight hours. Mary knew she had the supper ready. She could smell the beans baking and the brown bread steaming.

"I'm going to put on my old shoes and check that there's nothing out around the house and barn that might get blown away. You fill the woodbox."

"It's already full, Mother."

"Then put old newspapers on the floor, and pile extra wood on them. I have the mail with me, but I don't want to track in. I'll leave it here on the floor. You pick it up and put it on the sideboard."

A hired girl would be spoken to with more respect, Hattie Belle thought. If she'd known Lemmie would be gone so long, she would have accepted a teaching position so she'd be home only on weekends. But Lemmie had believed at first that he'd be home in time for a late August wedding.

She spread a clean white cloth over the table and placed the silver-plated castor set, with its cut glass bottles of vinegar, pepper, mustard and salt in the center of the table, and beside it a kerosene lamp. This time of year it got dark before one finished supper. From a three-sided, glassed-in china cupboard, built into a corner of the kitchen, she took the Blue Willow China her father had brought back from England when he was a young man. As always, she paused to admire the delicate Chinese designs of cobalt blue on a background of white.

Hattie Belle heard the side door open, then the rattle of the milk pails as Mary picked them up. "Bring me a pail of warm water," she called. "Your father's going to start milking. It looks really bad out there. Hope it won't do too much damage to the house."

When Hattie Belle brought the pail of warm water from the stove well, Mary added, "Who but fools would build a home on an iron ledge that runs out into the water?"

Is she calling everybody on this peninsula a fool? Hattie Belle asked herself. Probably so.

***

"When we were in Scotty, I had a nice talk with Zena Brown's sister, Cretia," Mary said, when she'd changed from her barn shoes and come into the kitchen. She paused in her account of Lemmie's aunt to put an apron over her navy blue serge suit, smooth back her thin brown hair, adjust her rimless glasses, and touch both small pearl earrings to ensure neither was loose. "Cretia said her brother Frank and his wife Delia will be arriving tomorrow. They're leaving Boston this evening on the overnight steamer *Portland*. They'll stay with Eph and Emma. Probably have a family gathering."

Hattie Belle smiled at the news. "How nice! I know they will all enjoy this chance to be together." She thought of the attractive couple and hoped she'd get to see them. In the summer, when they vacationed on the John's River side of the peninsula, they always came to Wednesday night prayer meetings at the old school house.

"Oh, but wait—" Hattie Belle said after a moment. "With the storm warnings out, the *Portland* most likely won't sail. They'll have to wait for better weather."

"I reckon that's the way t'will be," Captain Davis said as he came into the kitchen carrying a pail of milk in each hand.

Hattie Belle helped Mary strain the milk into pans, so the cream, after it rose to the top, could be skimmed off to make butter. Captain Davis removed his coat and hat, hung them behind the door, then sat down in his rocking chair and changed into his slippers. "Got so busy talking about the weather, Hattie Belle, didn't tell you I saw Joe Brown in Scotty."

"You did, Papa?"

"Ayuh. When I went to get Old John from the Metcalf Livery Stable. There he was—finishing one of his funny stories. His back was toward me, but I saw that red hair and knew that voice."

Hattie Belle pictured the livery stable—the harnesses hung on great hooks on the wall, the horses stamping in their stalls, a couple of men playing a serious game of checkers on the lid of a barrel, and the others enjoying the gossip and tall tales.

"Joe Brown! I said when the laughing stopped. He turned with a smile on his face, then stuck out his hand. 'Cap'n Davis!' he said. His one eyelid stays closed now, since that eye was taken out. But the good one is still full of the Old Nick. He asked about you, then letting on to be serious, swore that Lem wasn't half good enough for you."

Hattie Belle and Mary laughed at that, but Hattie Belle thought that Mary laughed too hard and long.

"How's the family, Joe? I asked.

"'Doing fine, Will,' he said. 'Percy is captain of Lawrence's old vessel, the two-master, *Addie E. Snow*, and Lawrence of the three-master, *Robert A. Snow.*'"

"So Percy is a captain now, too!" Hattie Belle said, her eyes glowing with pleasure.

"Ayuh.   Joe also said that Lawrence and Myrtie Belle are honeymooning on the *Robert A.* But we knew that. He and Zena think Percy and the newlyweds will be home for Christmas."

"Did you ask what they'd heard from Lemmie, Papa?"

"Ayuh. He'd written that a relief ship was due before Thanksgiving, probably the cruiser *Topeka*. Then the *Scorpion* will lose no time in pointing her nose north."

Hattie Belle nodded, her eyes thoughtful. Lemmie had said that in her letter, too—now if only the vessel can make it!

Sitting at the far side of the table, facing the windows, she watched the bronze haze disappear, and the tree branches begin to move with the wind. Was the storm, now moving into her life, the one that drove Lemmie's ship into the trough of the sea? If it took him, it might as well take her, too.

The food seemed to have no taste, but she forced herself to keep chewing and swallowing so as not to upset her father. She knew he worried that he might lose her to consumption, as he had her mother and her half-sister, May.

To keep herself from thinking about the coming gale, and the dream about the *Scorpion*, she tried to focus her thoughts on the Oriental romance revealed little by little on her plate as she ate.

As the helping of baked beans disappeared, she could see the cobalt blue palace, flanked by willows. Here the father imprisoned his beautiful daughter Koong Shee to keep her apart from his secretary Chang, the man she loved.

Glancing through the window, Hattie Belle saw the sky growing darker above the harbor, as the day came to an end.

Captain Davis noticed too, and reached to light the kerosene lamp beside the castor set.

Looking again at her plate, Hattie Belle moved her piece of brown bread, and saw the delicate blue bridge, over which the lovers raced. Beneath her spoonful of mustard pickles she saw the waiting boat, and behind it an island and the open sea.

When she lifted her eyes to look again through the window, she saw a full moon rising between dark clouds. Moonlit evenings with Lemmie were beautiful memories.

She glanced down at her plate, and gave her attention once again to the love story. She could almost hear her mother's voice as she said, "The couple managed to escape from her father and sail away. They had been gone but a little while, however, when a storm sprang up, and the small boat sank. They were lost at sea." The first time Hattie Belle heard the story, she had begun to cry. Then Mama pointed toward the top of the plate where two love birds flew side by side. "See? Those are the spirits of Koong Shee and Chang, Hattie Belle, and they live on to this very day."

"True love never dies," May added, and Hattie Belle, in childhood trust, had been sure that whatever her mother and sister said was right.

The memory of poor May's failed marriage pricked at the edges of her mind, trying to get her attention, but she pushed it away.

Picking up her blue-and-white china cup, which in days past had seemed to whisper endless tales of romance, she raised her eyes, to look above its delicate rim, and saw a dark cloud passing across the rising full moon.

Captain Davis, finished with his third cup of coffee, wiped around the edges of his mutton chop whiskers with his napkin, pushed back from the table, and crossed the room to where his three newspapers lay on a stand by the window. Hattie Belle had placed the newly arrived Boston and Portland dailies on top of the weekly Lincoln County News, published on Thursdays, yet because it carried local news, was re-read in part every day. He picked up the Portland paper and eased into his rocking chair.

Mary retired to the next room to sit in front of the fireplace and tat antimacassars—Christmas presents for her brothers and their wives.

"Going to be a humdinger, mark my words," Captain Davis said, nodding toward the outdoors. "A full moon makes heavy weather even worse. I remember a full moon the night we began sailing around the Cape—following the silk route to China. I was hardly more than a boy. We'd gone but a short distance when great gales shook the ship, heavy snow cut off our vision, and white water raged across the deck. The mate bawled out the names of those to stow a topsail in blinding snow. When I heard 'Davis,' I was terrified. I said all the prayers my mother ever taught me as I climbed the icy ratline. Half frozen, we pummeled and pulled for two hours, fearing at any moment we'd fall to our deaths."

She thought of the old saying, "He who would learn to pray, let him go to sea."

Her father had gone through a lot. She wondered what Lemmie was going through now. She wondered if he were still living.

Captain Davis filled the bowl of his Briar pipe with tobacco and tamped it down, and lit it. The aroma of the tobacco made her long for Lemmie. How she wished he hadn't had to sign up for the navy. It was strange how one evil person could change the course of another's life.

Hattie Belle remained at the table for awhile, listening to her father, and thinking about Lemmie, then stood up and started to remove the dirty dishes. Holding the cups and saucers in her hands, she moved across the room to stand by her father's rocking chair. "I can't stop worrying about Lemmie, Papa."

He looked up from his paper. "You've lived through bad times like this before. Remember two years ago when he was shipwrecked."

"Yes, I went through some bad days then." Hattie Belle carried the dirty dishes to the sink, filled the dishpan with hot water from the tank at the side of the wood stove, and thought of the last time she had seen Lemmie—in early April—more than half a year ago.

She was boarding with a family with whom she felt ill at ease. During the school year she stayed a short while in the homes of her various pupils. Most places were pleasant, but in this house she'd felt lonely.

When she received a letter from Lemmie which said he would be home from sea on April 4, a Monday, and visit her in her boarding house the next afternoon, she could hardly wait. That Tuesday, she hurried home from school and changed into her best dress, made of two different fabrics, the bodice of heavy blue and white silk, and the leg-o'-mutton sleeves and skirt of blue wool.

When she entered the landlady's fashionable parlor, she carried a tray which held a pot of tea, two cups and saucers trimmed in gold and cobalt blue, spoons, cream, sugar, napkins, and a plate of small currant drop cakes. The landlady followed her into the parlor. "Now, Miss Davis," she said, as she tucked a stray wisp of orange hair into place, "I'm too busy today to sit in here and be a chaperon, but I'll be close by. Your young man must follow house rules, and keep a respectable distance."

After the woman left, Hattie Belle sat down rather gingerly on a blue reception chair, which was part of a newly purchased four piece Turkish parlor suit. On the walls, in heavy oval frames, were portraits of the landlady's brothers and sisters. The women's piled-high hair held jeweled ornaments, and they wore a collection of gold chains around their necks. The men with their great walrus moustaches, sported fancy dress shirts with diamond studs.

A folded newspaper lay on the lower shelf of the parlor table, but she didn't look at it. As in every issue since Spain had blown up the *U.S.S. Maine* on February 15, there would be references to the infamous deed. She feared the oft written slogan, "Remember the *Maine*" was fanning national passions for war.

Hattie Belle heard quick footsteps on the piazza, and hurried to open the door. She shivered with delight as she saw him. He was even more handsome than she'd remembered.

"How's my girl?" he asked, his dark eyes smiling at her. He glanced toward the open door that led from the parlor into the dining room, and when he didn't see the landlady there, took Hattie Belle in his arms.

She'd waited for this for two months, but it seemed like forever.

The embrace could not be a long one, because if they were caught, Hattie Belle would be talked about. "Good news, Love," he whispered in her ear. "I've saved enough for us to get married. I'll be home next on the second Saturday in June. Let's get married the next day."

"Oh, Lemmie!" she'd said, tears in her eyes. "That sounds so good!"

She hung his navy blue top coat, bowler hat and scarf on the new hall tree, made of imitation mahogany. His clothes had the wonderful masculine smell of moustache wax, shaving soap, and pipe tobacco.

"Fancy furniture!" he commented, as he sat down in the red upholstered gents' easy chair. "Unfortunately," he said after a moment, "this piece was devised as an instrument of torture. The seat is of either brick or sandstone, I'm not sure which. Let's try sitting on the tete-a-tete. It looks more comfortable."

"I'd like that Lemmie, but the landlady has laid down the law. We're supposed to keep our distance from each other. Can I interest you in a cup of hot tea and a currant cake?"

"It's what I dreamed of those long, lonely nights at sea—tea and currant cake."

She poured the tea, and passed the cream and sugar. When she held out the plate of small cakes, he leaned forward to give her a kiss, but there was a firm cough from the doorway.

As they turned, they saw the edge of a grey wool skirt, and heard footsteps leading back to the kitchen.

He rolled his eyes toward the ceiling, then reached into his vest pocket for his match safe. As he lit his clay pipe, she saw the familiar anchor and shield tattoo at the base of his right thumb.

After a few moments, he took the pipe out of his mouth. "Here we are...a school teacher and a sea captain, treated like unruly children. It's ridiculous that we've had to wait so long to get married."

"It's been hard," she said. We might even have a child by now, she thought.

"We can thank the people at Green's Landing for these two wasted years." His jaw tightened.

"Just two and a half months till our wedding day," she said. "Thank goodness those days of waiting are almost past."

"Days badly spent, Hattie—days we should have been together. When the men were loading the *Sheepscot*, I said 'You're loading her too deep with stone.' But the owners kept insisting I take on more and more. I should have stood up to them and said 'NO.' They wouldn't have dared treat an older captain that way." He put his pipe back in his mouth and smoked in silence for awhile.

"If there is a bright side to the long wait, I was able to buy more things for the house...a churn, a sewing machine, curtains...."

He reached for her hand and squeezed it. "Good, Love." After a moment he returned to talking about the loss of the schooner. "They should have listened to me, and loaded her with a reasonable amount. If they had, the cargo wouldn't have broken loose. The pumps, running constantly, finally quit working. The men bailed day and night, but it was a losing battle." He stood up and paced about the room.

"We shouldn't have had to abandon her. I shouldn't have lost all my expensive instruments and charts or had to go into debt to replace everything. And we shouldn't have had this ridiculous long wait to get married."

His pipe had gone out, and he held the bit between his teeth, his eyes dark.

She hadn't seen this side of him before. "Bad times come to everyone, Lemmie, not just to us." He made no comment on what she'd said, and she wondered if he'd heard her.

He sat down and relit his pipe. "I have a lot of feelings tied up with the *Sheepscot*, Hattie. I often think, that if I'd never become captain of that vessel, and Frank had never become captain of the *Mavooshen*, he would be alive today."

"Don't talk about Frank, Lemmie, don't talk about Frank," she whispered. But he didn't hear.

He took a long swallow of tea, which had sat too long to be hot, and finished the small cake. "I got the *Sheepscot* about six weeks before we lost Frank. He went down on the *Mavooshen* in the February storm of '95."

"Yes," she whispered. The far-away look in his eyes told her he was going to talk about the loss of his older brother, and she wondered if she could bear to hear it. She nervously twisted her engagement ring, and rolled her lace edged handkerchief into a ball.

* * *

Hattie Belle rubbed her soapy dishcloth over a Blue Willow plate, and remembered what Lemmie had said about Frank and the way he had said it. Her keen memory was sometimes a blessing—sometimes not. It had been when she was a student at Gorham State Normal, studying to be a better teacher than just high school graduation allowed. She wished, however, that the words and pictures that went along with bitter-sweet times, would blur in her mind, the way they seemed to for others.

Lemmie had gone on talking in his characteristic way, saying part of what was on his mind, then pausing to draw on his pipe.

"Strange the way things happened, Hattie,...strange. In November of '94, I'd come into Boston in my old schooner, the *Sawyer*, and found a letter from Frank waiting for me at the shipping office."

Desperate to change the subject, Hattie Belle said, "Let's not think about the past, Lemmie." She got up and poured more tea into his cup, passed the sugar and cream, and put another cake on the side of his saucer. "Let's think about the future."

He nodded in agreement. But after she'd returned to her chair, he returned to his story, as if obsessed by it. "Frank wrote that the last time he'd come into Wiscasset, his vessel's home port, Richard Rundlett, the manager of the Maine Shipbuilding and Navigation Company had called him into his office. Mr. Rundlett told Frank that his next vessel was to be the three masted *Mavooshen*. Frank then asked if I could be captain of his old schooner, the two masted *Sheepscot*.

"The manager, who knew I'd been a captain since the age of nineteen, agreed. The pay would be higher than what I had been getting on the

Sawyer and the *Sheepscot* was in much better condition. Frank had been trying for months to get a better schooner for me."

Hattie Belle's head throbbed. If only he'd stop talking about Frank. The people in the pictures along the walls irritated her. Everyone of them looked like the landlady.

"My brother ended his letter by saying he'd be home around the eighth of December. If I could manage to be there, too, we could visit with the folks for a few days. Then we'd go on to Wiscasset together."

Captain Davis looked up from his newspaper. "I hope the young skippers in port tonight will stay there, and not try, out of pride, to make their schedules. I remember disregarding the weather warnings a couple of times at first. Almost lost my schooner and my life."

"I do hope they'll be cautious," Hattie Belle said. After a few minutes her thoughts returned to the fancy parlor and the last time she'd seen the handsome man she loved.

When he'd paused for a while, holding the pipe in the palm of his hand, she had tried to think of something to say, to change the subject. Before she could, he'd begun again, this time in a low and halting voice, as if he didn't want to tell the story, but something inside wouldn't let him alone until he did.

"That first night at home, Frank and I were sitting with Father in front of the fireplace, smoking, when I noticed how quiet Frank sat, just staring into the flames. Father had begun telling one of his tall tales, but my brother paid him no mind. He seemed to be listening to his own thoughts."

Captain Lemuel Brown and Hattie Belle

Hattie Belle could picture the Brown's big kitchen, with Lemmie, Frank, and their father sitting in front of the big brick fireplace, smoking. She could see the scene more clearly than she wanted to.

"After Frank had sat for a piece, he turned to me and said, 'Lem, we're in a hard and dangerous business. If anything should happen to me, and I saw, from the other side, that you were in trouble, I'd help you if I could.'"

Even though Hattie Belle's hands were in hot soapy water, an icy chill ran through her as she remembered hearing those words.

Lemmie had stopped talking to take a draw on his pipe. At length he took it out of his mouth. "Frank took off in the buggy a couple of times—didn't want me to go with him. I teased him about having a girlfriend. He grinned and said I might be right."

Hattie Belle looked out the window, determined not to listen. But Lemmie kept on talking. She tried to turn her thoughts to other things, such as the blue satin suit she'd just made for her trousseau, and what Lemmie would say when he saw her in it, but she couldn't block out the words he was saying now.

"A couple of days later, Frank and I started off for Wiscasset. He seemed like his old self, and made no more mention of what he had said that first night we were home. It was as if he'd never said it.

"I quit worrying about it and enjoyed being in that pretty town with its big white houses. Most are owned by master mariners. One day we walked down to the grandest of them all, Castle Tucker. It commands the point overlooking Wiscasset Harbor.

"On December 15th, the company, as promised, made me captain of Frank's old vessel, the *Sheepscot*, and gave him the *Mavooshen*. On Sunday we went to church, then wrote letters home. Frank also wrote to his girlfriend. He still wouldn't tell me her name, but promised I'd know before long. I never did find out. Well, I guess it isn't that important."

It is to me, Lemmie, she said silently.

He took a draw on his pipe, then waited a minute before he spoke again. "I learned from the folks that after a couple of weeks had passed, Frank sent them a letter from Philadelphia, dated January 30. He said that his schooner had been loaded with coal, and he planned to leave the next day for Wiscasset. He'd promised to write again as soon as he made port."

Captain Davis had put down his newspaper for a bit, and was looking out the window, watching dark clouds moving across the full moon. "I wonder when the storm will strike. I remember how I always dreaded heavy snow at sea. It was like a curtain coming down in front of my eyes. There were always the fog bells, the whistling buoys, and the compass to rely on. I was still mighty uneasy."

"I pray the storm won't be too bad, Papa," she said.

She remembered that Lemmie had drawn pictures in the air with the stem of his pipe ... great half circles of wind coming up the coast, then small half-circles to signify the rough passage of the *Mavooshen*.

"When the sky and sea grew a bit less ugly," he said, "the *Mavooshen* weighed anchor and started on her voyage. Old salts told me that the schooner, encrusted with ice, rounded Cape May and headed north. I couldn't find out anything else for certain. But a Captain Freese, who during the storm was bringing a steamer north from Demerara, said that no small vessel could have lived in such a sea." He took a deep breath. "We never saw Frank again."

"I know," Hattie Belle said in a faint voice. "I know." She didn't realize that tears were streaming from her eyes until Lemmie leaned over to gently wipe her face with his handkerchief and gave her a tender hug.

He had told her then how hard it was to keep sailing on the *Sheepscot*, because in his mind she was always Frank's schooner. "I slept in his bunk, shaved in front of his mirror, and read the magazines and books he'd left me."

"Look out there, Hattie Belle," Captain Davis cried. "In the moonlight you can see that the wind is churning the water white—never saw the likes in this harbor. I'm fearful for those vessels out there, especially the *Chamberlain*."

Her hands full of clean dishes, she was walking toward the china cabinet, but paused beside her father to look out the window. "Oh! Terrible!" she said. The winds must be from the hurricane coming up from the Caribbean, the one in her nightmare.

She opened the glass door and laid the dishes on the shelves. A fan with a painted bull fight scene, sent by Lemmie from Cuba, stood open on the top shelf. She wondered if he were still alive. No, she mustn't let herself think that way. Her thoughts returned to that last day she had seen him.

"It was only a few months after we'd lost Frank that his prediction came true," Lemmie said.

Hattie Belle had fiddled with her ring and twisted her damp Sunday handkerchief into a knot. She had prayed that she could keep her composure as he told the story.

Lemmmie shifted in his chair. "While on a run south, there came up heavy squalls of wind, which blew us off course. The schooner rolled heavily and shipped seas forward and aft. About midnight the lashings of the seas grew calmer. Having spent endless watches at the wheel, I left the steering to the mate and staggered below. I'd fallen sound asleep, when suddenly I heard Frank's voice shout loud and clear, 'Hard-a-lee!'

"I sprang from my bunk, and as my feet hit the boards, I screamed it into the night, 'Hard-a-lee!'

"The mate heard, and in that instant came wide awake, and began turning the vessel completely about. I began running up the companionway. As I reached the deck, the curtain of the storm lifted. Looking back over my shoulder, I could see for a few seconds, the great black and white striped lighthouse of Hatteras sending

Capt. Frank Brown

its beam out into the storm ... and I could see the bones of schooners caught forever on the sandbars."

In spite of her resolution not to cry again, she felt the tears coming, and dabbed at her eyes with the soggy handkerchief.

"You know, Hattie, people always said Frank reminded them of Father, probably because both had red hair. But he had Mother's and Grandmother Stevens's gifts. He could tell the future from dreams. Thinking back on that night we sat in front of the kitchen hearth, and remembering the strange look on his face, I think he knew then that his time was near."

No, Lemmie, she said silently. He was very depressed that evening because he had received news of a friend's death at sea. Other than that, December of '94 was the happiest time of his life. He said so twice.

She wanted to tell Lemmie right then that she was the girl Frank visited, the girl he wrote to from Wiscasset, saying, "I'll buy you a ring in Philadelphia, then we'll announce our engagement to the world." But she didn't want to hurt him.

The last time she'd seen Frank was when he rode into the school yard at the end of the day—the day before he left for Wiscasset. She had been coming down the steps, her arms full of papers. They stood together under the big oak tree. 'Wait for me, Hattie?' he asked, and when she said she would, he kissed her, a long, lingering kiss to last them through the months they'd be apart. The papers slipped to the ground.

When he was lost at sea, she'd fallen ill with grief. She couldn't talk about it—didn't want people feeling sorry for her, gossiping about their lost love.

The only person who knows is your mother, Lemmie, she thought. I asked her not to tell and she swore to keep our secret forever!

Chapter 6

East Boston

Delia

Delia awakened to the mournful cry of the fog horn, and when she thought of what the day would bring, the doleful sound seemed to echo her own state of mind.

Frank stayed asleep, his full, dark beard, against her honey-blonde hair. Careful not to wake him, she lifted his arm from around her and inched out from beneath it and the heavy quilts. Shivering in the cold, she hurried to the edge of the fringed rug and pulled back the lace curtains.

A small woman, about five feet tall, with hair that was long enough to sit on, she stayed for a while at the window. She wore a lace trimmed nightgown that clung to her hour-glass figure.

Her pale green eyes looked out at the sea fog that had rolled in off the ocean. It softened the edges of the house next door, and erased the lumber company's factories and planing mills beyond. There was no view of the sky, no chance to read its forecast for the day. She had been praying for heavy weather to prevent them from taking the trip she dreaded.

(Courtesy of the Society for the Preservation of New England Antiquities)
The PORTLAND Photograph by N.L. Stebbins

Her husband, Frank, a big, handsome man who worked as a stevedore on the wharves of East Boston had, without her knowledge, bought tickets for the overnight steamer, *Portland*. The 211 foot sidewheeler was due to leave Boston's India Wharf at 7 p.m. and arrive at Portland, Maine the next morning. From there they would have to travel by train, ferry, and stagecoach to reach the village of Pemaquid Harbor where most of his people lived, including the sisters who actively disliked her.

Frank had sprung the dreadful surprise last Sunday, on their way home from church in their carriage. Before he spoke, she had been in a happy mood, enjoying glimpses of white capped water, as various wharves provided open spaces between the factories and shops. Just as she began removing her wide brimmed hat with the ribbons and rosettes, to keep it from blowing away with the wind, he said it.

"I have a treat for you, Deal. I've got tickets on the *Portland* for this coming Saturday. We'll be in Pemaquid Harbor for an early Christmas. I know how much you love it there."

Immediately she thought of what she would have to endure from his sisters and felt sick to her stomach. She forgot to hold onto her hat, and almost lost it. She and Frank always vacationed in Pemaquid Harbor in the summer, but that was entirely different. The presence of her sister's son, Don, and his family, who vacationed there also, protected her from Frank's sisters' mean remarks or scathing glances.

"I think we're making a mistake to visit your people now," Delia had said in her whispery voice, as he reined up the horses in front of the barn. "It's beautiful there in June, July and August, but then it starts to get cold. Nobody goes there at this time of year."

"They don't know what they're missing," he'd said, as he lifted her down from the carriage, gave her a kiss, and an affectionate squeeze to her little waist. "It's as pretty there in the winter as it is in the summer, Deal. But instead of rowing across the river and picnicking, we'll go ice skating in the moonlight then roast chestnuts in the fireplace."

Now she could hear the sound of horses clopping by the house as their owners took them to the blacksmith shop, which would open at seven. She had the desperate feeling that she had no more control over her life than those animals did.

Exactly on the hour, the loud tooting of factory whistles began, signalling that the working man's day had begun.

Frank threw back the quilts and jumped to his feet. As he did, Sheba, Delia's big yellow cat, sprang from the foot of their bed, with a sharp cry of complaint at being disturbed.

"The big day is here, Deal," Frank said, as he came to give her a hug and kiss. "I'll go out and tend to the horses, then tighten up around the house and barn."

It wasn't until the middle of the morning that the fog burned off and gave her a clear view of the sky. There were clouds, but none very dark or threatening.

While packing the first two valises, she stopped several times to hurry across the bedroom rug, pull back the curtains, and check the sky above the buildings. It remained the same.

But there were other signs that gave Delia hope. Shortly after the noon meal, she became quite sure that a dramatic change in the weather was on the way. When she stepped out on the piazza to shake the biscuit crumbs from the kitchen tablecloth, she was surprised to find the air felt quite different from the way it usually did at that time of year. Because East Boston was really an island in Boston Harbor, she had expected late November winds carrying a damp chill from the water. Today, however, she felt a brooding calm, with air as cold as liquid ice.

In the late afternoon, she stood in front of the bedroom looking-glass, fastened her gold watch to the jacket of her travel suit, and pinned a garnet ornament into her elaborately styled hair. Still only a touch of grey, thank goodness.

She began packing the last of their three valises. The heavy weather had to come soon, or it would be too late to prevent their trip. In a few hours she could be aboard the *Portland*, on her way to that dreadful visit in Maine.

She pictured the desolate appearance that the John's River side of the mile-wide peninsula would have at this time of year: the pine and fir trees heavy with snow, the river iced over, the few summer cottages along its banks standing empty. The only sign of life would be the smoke curling up from the chimneys of the three white houses, each occupied by a Stevens.

In the summer, when she was sure of her relatives' presence, she could relax and enjoy being on the beautiful little peninsula. In fact, she looked forward to that first glimpse of John's River. When they came to the top of the hill in the buggy, she would see with great pleasure the blue-green water rippling along, and their pretty little summer home along its edge. To the near left of their place sat the cottage where her nephew Don and his family vacationed.

Frank pushed back the chenille portiere that hung in the archway between the downstairs bedroom and the kitchen. "Just came in for that last piece of apple pie. I've got more work to do outside. How are you coming with the packing?"

"All right, I guess."

"If I know Eph, he'll be planning a family get-together for us," Frank said, his eyes glowing with pleasure at the thought. "Don't forget to pack those presents."

Delia shuddered at the thought of a Stevens gathering without any of her own people present. She could deal with an afternoon visit at Cretia's or Euda's, with tea and molasses cookies served, and Frank sitting right beside her. But when everyone came together, it meant the preparation of big meals, and being alone in the kitchen with the women. Frank would be in another room, with the men, smoking and spinning yarns.

She turned to look at the row of brooches laid out on the dresser. The prettiest one would go to Eph's sweet wife, Emma, who never said a bad word about anyone.

Delia could hear Frank open the pie safe's squeaky door. "Where are those buckskin tobacco pouches you got for the men?" she asked, raising her voice so Frank could hear her in the kitchen.

"Top right hand drawer," he called back. "And I plan to give a half dollar apiece to the young people."

She knew the money would be received with joy by the nieces and nephews, but the parents would receive their gifts with a mixture of pleasure and envy. They were jealous that Frank was so prosperous, while they had to work from dawn till dusk to wrest a living from the sea and rocky land.

Cretia could be counted on to say, "Running whiskey from Canada, are you, Frank?" They would all laugh heartily at the joke, and Frank would laugh along with them. Then there would be a little space of quietness while they looked at him, waiting, but he never explained, and neither did she. In truth, Frank and a wealthy cousin were partners in a ship's chandlery in South Boston. Although hired help managed the store, enough divided profit remained to give Frank a fairly good income. He also had his pay as a stevedore, responsible for loading and unloading big schooners and steamers that came and went from the wharves of East Boston.

Delia could hear the kitchen door open and close.

She cast about in her mind again and again to find some way to keep from going to Pemaquid Harbor. His sisters' dislike of her had grown much worse since the death of their niece, May.

"They blame me for everything that happened," she said aloud, although there was no one to hear but the cat as she rubbed against Delia's ankles. "You'd think it was my idea to have her work in the factory and tire herself out."

While she wrapped the tobacco pouches in gift paper, she thought about how both she and Frank had begged May not to work in that sweat shop. "You're here to go to college," he said, "not wear yourself out doing piece work. Let us help you."

May shook her head "no." She had that crazy "Stevens pride."

"If you want, we'll call it a loan," Frank said, "and you can pay it back a little at a time." He held out the money, but she wouldn't take it.

When May was at work, Delia went into her bedroom and laid the bills on her dresser, but she wouldn't pick them up...just let them lay there. Finally, when the child began looking quite tired, but still insisted on working, Delia and Frank, in desperation, went to the factory. They found her among the crowd of pale, over-worked young women, and demanded that she come home with them.

Frank's sisters didn't know how much she and Frank loved that child. When May died, they cried for days and Frank grieved so much he couldn't go to work. Her death hit him hard, even harder than the loss of his namesake at sea.

She began wrapping the brooches, but felt like throwing away those she'd bought for his sisters. They didn't deserve a gift, blaming her the way they did, for everything that happened. If there was any blame to be given out, why didn't Frank's sister Zena, May's mother, share it? Why had she sent that child to the city without enough money for books and tuition, and in clothes that weren't right for a girl who would be mingling with the daughters of wealthy merchants?

Delia had decided never to say those things aloud, as they would cause a great rift in the family that could never be healed. Yet, it seemed terribly unfair to be blamed for a lack of caring, because it was completely untrue. She had tried to explain, but they wouldn't listen. After that, there was nothing to do but bear the icy looks and a variety of mean comments.

One sister made a cruel remark last summer during a Stevens family gathering at Eph's. Euda sat in her wheelchair in a corner of the kitchen, while Emma, Cretia and Delia prepared the meal. The nephew, Don, and family had been invited, but had gone sight-seeing at Fort William Henry. With the dinner almost ready, frail Emma said she believed she'd have to lie down for a bit.

Delia decided to slip out to the backhouse for a moment. She had barely closed the kitchen door behind her, when she heard one of them say in a loud voice, "Poor Frank, he has had two bad marriages. Neither woman could give him a child. Everyone knows that what a man wants most is a son to carry on his name."

Someone was rapping on the bedroom window.

"Do you hear me, Deal?" Frank shouted.

She pulled back the lace curtain. "Your brother, George, just drove by. Didn't have time to stop and visit. Said he'd take good care of the horses and house while we're gone."

"Fine!" she shouted back. She tucked several pairs of heavy winter underwear into the valise, to wear one over the other when icy winds blew—long sleeved undershirts, ankle length ribbed drawers, black cashmere stockings, and a couple of flannel petticoats.

The Pemaquid Harbor peninsula was farther north than East Boston, so it stood to reason it would be even colder, as cold as his sisters.

She didn't suppose Frank's younger brother, Lem, and his family could come from Rockland, or Zena and her family from Walpole. She'd heard people there tell that they didn't like to travel any distance in winter weather. Even if the roads were clear when they left, a storm could hit on the way, or come up after they arrived, and cause them to be snowed in.

Oh, it was crazy for Frank to want to go there at this time of year.

She heard the kitchen door open again. He stuck his head into the bedroom. "Going to fix a little something to eat before we leave?"

Pushing aside the portiere, Delia stepped into the kitchen. "It has to be leftovers, Frank. There isn't time to cook." After a few minutes, she placed on the table before him a plate with sandwiches made of leftover beef and biscuits. She poured him a cup of reheated coffee. "When our cottage was being built, why didn't you have the men put in enough

insulation for winter living? Then we could be on our own and wouldn't
have to stay with Eph and Emma."

"Didn't think of it at the time. But don't worry, Deal, they'll be glad
to have us. And it will give me a lot of time to chew the fat with Eph."

She put a sandwich on her own plate. "That leaves me with Emma,
and her postcard collection," she said, as she reached for a cup. "Your
sisters don't like me."

"Well, you do have some serious faults, Deal," he said.

"What?" she asked in alarm, almost dropping the cup. She quickly
moved to stand beside his chair. "You've got to tell me. I'll try to
change."

"First off, there is this 'crowning glory,'" he said, gesturing toward
the thick, piled high blonde hair. He reached out to tweak one of the little
corkscrew curls above her forehead. He cupped calloused fingers beneath
her chin. "Then there is this pretty face that looks like a picture on a
magazine cover." Putting both big hands at either side of her waist, so that
his thumbs and forefingers almost touched, he added, "Could be your worst
fault is this hour-glass figure."

"Oh Frank! How you do carry on!"

"My sisters are good women, but they're plain. I expect they don't
like it the way their husband's eyes light up when you come into a room."
He laughed then, and pulled her onto his lap. "It's the curse of a beautiful
woman," he whispered in her ear.

Delia realized that unless a combination of heavy winds and snow
churned into Boston Harbor soon, there was little hope she could escape
from going to Maine.

"Hey!" Frank suddenly shouted, snapping his napkin on the table. "Look at your crazy cat. She's after your food."

"Sheba! Shoo! Shoo!" Delia cried as she jumped off Frank's lap. But the cat was quick. She sprang from the table to the floor, the meat in her mouth, and ran behind the stove.

"Oh dear! I've been so busy packing that I forgot to feed her. Well, I'll let her finish, then take her next door to May Belle's. She promised to look after kitty while we're gone."

After Delia knocked on the neighbor's door, her plump and pretty friend appeared and held out her arms for the cat. As usual, she was worried about something, and all frowned up. "Have you heard that the lumber company is going to be sold at auction, Delia?" she asked. "Richard keeps saying how lucky we are that he has his own fishing boat and doesn't have to be at the mercy of a big business."

Delia hoped, for sentimental reasons, that whoever bought it would leave the big lumber wharf exactly as it was. If it hadn't been there, when she'd first moved to East Boston, she and Frank wouldn't have met.

She liked to take time out from her daily walks, to stand for a moment or two on the exact spot on Condor Street where they were introduced. She had been 21 that summer of '70, newly divorced, and gossiped about by her neighbors in St. John, New Brunswick.

Anxious to get away from the pain of having old-time friends look the other way when they met her on the street, she left Canada and came to the United States to visit her brother George and his wife.

Delia secretly hoped she would find someone who would marry her. Her mother had warned her, though, there was little chance any decent man would want to wed a divorced woman. Her dreams were kinder. A heartbreakingly handsome dark haired man appeared in them night after night, and each time slipped a gold ring on the third finger of her left hand.

Late one summer afternoon her dream began to come true. She and her brother were walking past the shops and factories along the waterfront. She wore her blue street gown, made of China silk, and carried a matching parasol. "I do need to get out in the air," she'd told George when he came home from town, "and of course I can't go by myself."

They were passing the entrance to the wharf, when a large number of men who worked at the lumber company were leaving for the day. "Frank!" her brother called out, and a handsome man with jet black hair and beard turned his head, and started across the street toward them. How tall he is! she thought, probably about 6 feet, a good foot taller than I am.

"He's a good fellow," George said to her under his breath. "Sings in the church choir—lost his wife not too long ago." As the young man came closer, she recognized him, and almost fainted. He was the person in her dreams, the man who night after night had slipped a gold ring on her finger.

After a six month courtship, she and Frank married and eventually bought the place on Falcon Street.

As Delia returned to her packing, she still felt like throwing away the gifts for Frank's sisters. She resisted, however, and stuck the wrapped brooches in between her two flannel petticoats to protect them from being chipped. Her arguments about not going to Maine had been useless, and the weather hadn't changed.

But when Delia looked up after closing the valise, she saw a difference in the light that came sifting through the lace curtains. A strange bronze color had spread across the sky above the buildings of the lumber company. Immediately she had a twinge of guilt. In her prayers for a bit of heavy weather, nothing that bad had been visualized. A hurricane must be coming.

"Oh dear!" Delia said aloud. "I'll have to tell Frank." No question now, of course, about cancelling the trip to Maine.

She pulled aside the portiere. "Look out the window at the sky, Frank. We'll have to put off our trip to Maine."

"I've already looked, Deal." He was polishing his colt skin shoes, which sat on old newspapers laid on the seat of a kitchen chair. "We'll go on down to India Wharf and see what people there think."

"I don't know, Frank...."

"I tell you, Deal, if there is the least sign of a blow, that sidewheeler will hug the dock. It has happened so often that we stevedores call the Boston and Portland Steam Packet the old granny line."

"What is the use of going down there then, Frank? We've seen that warning light."

She saw his lips form a stubborn line, and remembered her first husband's mouth set in the exact same way. That union had lasted only 12 months. She and Frank had been wed for twenty-eight years, but she knew certain arguments were to be avoided.

I must be careful of what I say, she told herself. She nervously picked a small piece of lint from a green velvet lapel on her black broadcloth suit jacket. "On the other hand, I suppose it couldn't hurt to see what those at the wharf think."

His expression softened. "You look beautiful in your new outfit, Deal. The green part on your jacket matches your eyes." A mischievous smile turned up the corners of his bearded lips, and his eyes seemed to dance. "With that gold watch on your jacket, that big pendant hanging from the chain around your neck, the garnet eardrops and the diamond rings, you look too pretty for a wife. People will think you're my fancy woman. I kind of like that."

"Oh Frank!" Although her stomach was churning with worry about the trip to Maine, she had to smile at his nonsense. She returned to the bedroom, and sitting on the chair, took off her house shoes and put on fashionable high cut Button Gaiters with gum soles, jersey cloth tops and fleece lining, an attractive protection against the cold.

She would go along with Frank's idea, which made no sense to her, and say nothing else. When they got down to the wharf, he would see that the *Portland* wasn't going to sail, and they'd come right back home again. He acted as if she didn't know anything about weather and water. Wasn't she from St. John, on the Bay of Fundy, where the highest tides in the world were? The treachery of wind and water were the main topics of conversation.

She stood on the little step stool that Frank had made for her, so that she could reach the high closet shelf, and lifted down a large hat box. Then she pushed back the portiere with an elbow, and backed into the kitchen.

Still upset, she decided she needed to make a cup of tea to calm herself. When she was growing up in St. John, her mother had always insisted that after a cup of the steaming brew one could better face the problems of the day.

Delia saw the clock said 4:30, so there was time. The cab wasn't due until five.

"Tea, Frank?"

He shook his head.

She took the lid from the tea canister, then dropped a tablespoonful of its dried leaves into her favorite cup, the one with the country scene from the Emerald Isle. Her father had brought it with him when he came to St. John from Ireland. She poured in hot water from the kettle on the coal stove.

Frank had buffed his shoes until they shone. Now he took off his plaid shirt and overalls and got into his best clothes...a white shirt with wing collar, and a grey wool suit, with black velvet lapels. He stood in front of the looking glass, lifted his bearded chin, then turned it sideways to make sure his black bow tie was straight.

The hot water in her cup had turned amber, and she began to sip the soothing liquid. After just a few swallows, she felt herself relaxing.

As Frank moved away from the looking glass, Delia watched him admiringly over the rim of her teacup. Although he was big, deep chested, and muscular, he walked with an easy grace. She liked his swarthy skin, too. "My mother was part Penobscot Indian," he'd told her. "I see the high check bones, different shaped eyes, and dark skin on a lot of the down east people. Like me, they had an ancestor who came from Europe in the early days, and married an Indian woman."

He seemed to grow even better looking as he got older. When with him on the street or in a restaurant, she fancied she could see other women looking at him admiringly.

Delia took another sip of tea. When about a quarter of an inch of liquid remained, she decided to read the leaves. She walked over to the sink, and swirled the leaf and liquid mixture around the inside of the cup, letting it tip enough so that water sloshed over the top. When the liquid was gone, and the leaves clung to the inside of the cup, she returned to the table, and set the cup upside down in the saucer.

While she rotated it in a clockwise direction, she thought of how ridiculous and really wasteful it was to pay a cabby to take them down to India Wharf, then to have to hire another to bring them right back home.

When she picked up the cup and looked inside, expecting to see a scattering of leaves, she saw they had grouped into two symbols. They were directly to the left of the handle and near the rim. It meant that whatever was predicted would happen soon.

Delia turned the cup to better see what the symbols were. When she saw them, her mouth went dry and she began to tremble. The first grouping had taken the form of a schooner, and the one beside it, a coffin.

Immediately she had a misty vision of a violent storm at sea. She could see two vessels. One, a small schooner, with broken masts, and the other, which she could hardly make out, seemed to be a great steamer, rolling and pitching heavily, with its superstructure damaged. On the deck of the schooner, a young man in oilskins struggled with the wheel. The broken masts beat against the side of the schooner. As she watched, a great wave lifted the little vessel and slammed her into the crippled steamer. The schooner disappeared from sight. The big steamer seemed to be breaking apart, and she could hear passengers screaming.

The scene vanished as suddenly as it had appeared.

Feeling faint, she grabbed onto the edge of the table. The vision had been so frightening, so powerful.... She ought to tell Frank what she had seen, but she had become too shaken, too overcome with emotion, to say anything.

She heard the clop of a horse's hooves and the creak of carriage wheels as the cab came into the yard, lanterns glowing on either side.

Moving slowly, almost as if in a trance, she removed the cover from the box on the table and lifted out her hat with its tufts of egret feathers, pheasant plumes and ribbon. From habit, she reached for the array of hat pins, kept on a shelf above the looking-glass.

Frank, now in his overcoat and bowler hat, tossed her astrakhan lamb cape around her shoulders, dropped the matching muff into her hands, and propelled her out the door.

Chapter 7

India Wharf

"It's India Wharf now, is it?" the poorly dressed cabby asked, as he picked up the three valises.

"Right," Frank said. "We're sailing on the *Portland* at seven."

"Would you be knowing there's a red flag flying over the post office? Heavy gales are on the way, and that's for sure."

Frank smiled. "I'm not worried about the weather."

Because Delia had to lift her skirt a bit to climb into the cab, Frank positioned himself so that in the moonlight the driver wouldn't get a glimpse of her ankles.

After she was seated, Frank continued his conversation with the cabby. "The *Portland's* owners are old grannies," he said. "If they think there is any danger at all, the steamer won't sail."

"The Saints be praised," the cabby said.

Because Delia was shivering, Frank pulled the carriage curtain closed and tucked the lap robe around her.

He didn't know that she shivered because of emotion as she relived the vision of the two doomed vessels at sea. How she wished she hadn't seen it!

The visions had begun years ago, when Delia was a little girl. There had been a storm one night, with loud crashes of thunder. She had awakened frightened and crying, and snuggled close to her older sister Patience for protection. That next morning, when she heard her mother and father worry aloud about a lost lamb, she piped, "I know where it is. It's caught between two rocks ... down near the water. I can see the picture in my head." Although her ten older brothers and sisters laughed and hooted, they found the lamb just where she led them. On freeing the frightened little creature, Delia's father declared, "It's second sight you have, child, a blessed gift."

That day the gift proved to be a blessing, but there were many other times, like today, when she wished to be free of it. She couldn't change what she had just seen, so the vision remained an unbearable burden on her mind.

On the ride to the South Ferry the tea-leaf prophesy of imminent death, and the vision of broken and sinking vessels at sea stayed constantly on her mind. Only when the carriage came to a stop, did she become aware of her surroundings.

Frank paid at the toll collector's house, and the carriage moved onto the boat. A ferry left East Boston every few minutes for the third of a mile crossing to the mainland. Delia usually enjoyed that short ride across the water, but tonight, as she and Frank went inside and sat down near a window, she found herself too full of worry to enjoy anything.

They looked out at vessels in the harbor, then across to the city of Boston. Frank, in an excellent mood, said, "In the moonlight, I believe I can make out the old North Church steeple. A really important part of the Revolution got played out there! Can't you picture the sexton climbing into the steeple and hanging two lanterns to signal that the British were moving up the Charles River? 'One if by land, two if by sea.' Remember? They'll have a big celebration here this coming weekend, Deal, the one hundred twenty fifth anniversary. Kind of wish we were going to be around for it."

"Yes, Frank." No use reminding him again that she had grown up in Canada and had altogether different heroes.

Now he stared intently at the vessels in the harbor. "There are a couple of foreign ships out there, Deal," he said, his voice alive with interest.

She made no comment.

After they landed, the ride from ferry slip to broad Atlantic Avenue took only a few minutes, then they rode parallel to Boston Harbor. The sound of the horse's hooves echoed on the cobblestone street. When she tried to look out through the isinglass window, the full moon appeared to be only a blur of light in the sky. But coming across on the ferry, she had seen a misty ring around it, which meant either rain or snow; given the chill of the evening, probably snow.

Within a few minutes the driver called out, "Sure and it's India Wharf now."

Frank paid the fellow the $2.50 fare and, although tipping was considered a decadent old-world custom, added $.25.

"The Saints protect you, sir," the cabby said, touching his threadbare cap.

(Courtesy of the Society for the Preservation of New England Antiquities)
Noodle Island Ferry (East Boston)

(Courtesy of the Society for the Preservation of New England Antiquities)

Merchants standing in front of India Wharf Warehouse

The huge brick warehouse on the right side of the wharf loomed up before them. To its left, travelers saying goodby to friends and relatives formed groups in front of the several steamers moored along the pier. Longshoremen carried barrels and boxes from nearby railroad cars to the ships; young sailors laughed and talked among themselves.

Delia struggled to keep up with her husband's long strides as they walked by shops, catering to mariners, at the wharf level of the warehouse. When passing one with the sign, "Ship Bottoms Repaired, & Salvage," she glanced toward the door, and saw two longshoremen, who had stopped for a smoke, staring at her appreciatively.

The air felt cold and damp, but the usual waterfront wind was missing.

Although business along the waterfront went on as usual, she saw concern on the faces of some of the old sailors, who idled about the wharf in patched clothes, smoking their corncob pipes. Three, who stood looking out onto the moonlit path across Boston Harbor, were shaking their heads and muttering. As she and Frank passed close by, she heard one of them say to his friends, "I tell you, after seeing that yellow sky, nobody but a fool would put to sea tonight."

She glanced up at Frank, but he gave no sign he had heard.

They soon joined the group of people waiting to board the *Portland*. Frank's eyes shone with pleasure at the sight of the elegant gold trimmed white sidewheeler. The big ship, which had been wired for electricity, seemed to light up the harbor. "What a beauty!" he said. "I guess I don't blame the owners for being so fussy about her."

Delia nodded, only half-listening. Her mind was again on the vision of the sailor tied to the wheel of the schooner with the broken masts, and the mist-enveloped liner that was breaking apart.

Frank continued to stare at the *Portland* in admiration. "She's known for serving great suppers. Can't wait to taste that steamship round of beef again, and those great pies."

Delia nodded and tried to smile. As the air grew colder, she turned up her collar, thankful for the warmth of the fur.

"I have a surprise for you, Deal," Frank said. "I managed to get us a stateroom with its own washbowl and pitcher, and instead of bunks we've got us a poster bed. What do you think of that!"

Delia knew there was no way she could talk him out of sailing. She swallowed hard, then managed to whisper, "That was so dear of you, Frank."

He gave her a mischievous grin. "I heard a new story I'll tell you later. It's about a peg-legged captain and a mermaid."

The gangplank was in place now, and several passengers were boarding amid shouts of farewell. Some were smiling, but several looked worried. The wind blew stronger and a light snow began.

"The ship is going to sail tonight, for sure," Frank said, as he watched the people boarding. "That means the owners aren't worried about the weather, and Captain Blanchard isn't either. The storm must have changed course. Well, get out the tickets, and let's climb aboard."

She looked down at her hands expecting to see the small leather bag in which she carried her valuables, but saw that she carried only her muff.

"My purse, Frank...my purse! Where is it? Oh no! I must have left it on the kitchen table."

"Delia! How could you!"

"Oh, I'm so sorry, Frank."

As tears filled her eyes, he said, "Forget it. I'll get a fast cab home and be back in no time."

His words were kind, but she felt his anger.

Delia stood to the right of the gangplank, the three brown leather valises at her feet, and watched her husband running down the wharf toward Atlantic Avenue. She wondered if he could make it back before the *Portland* sailed.

How could she have forgotten the tickets? Then she remembered the state of shock she had been in when the cab came, and the way Frank had hurried her out the door.

Two well dressed men, who appeared to be merchants, stood not far away looking out into the harbor. "Did you hear about the wire from the weather bureau?" the short fellow asked.

"I did," the taller one said. "I'm glad I didn't send off my sawed lumber and masts to the West Indies, the way I'd planned to."

"Right," the short fellow agreed. "To tell the truth, I'm surprised the *Portland* is still scheduled to sail at seven. I heard that Charles Williams, the passenger agent, got a telephone call from the manager, who told him to tell Captain Blanchard to wait for a weather report at nine. I'll bet the captain didn't get the message."

"You could be right about that. Blanchard is a cautious man. I heard this past week the owners called him in and told him they were tired of his not leaving when they told him to, that from now on he has to follow orders. Don't know if there's any truth in it. This is the world's worst place for rumors."

"Well, whatever did or didn't happen, Captain Blanchard has a right to be cautious. I don't envy him his job. A lot of people think the *Portland* is the safest vessel around, but I don't agree. Sidewheelers have too shallow a draft to suit me. They're good on rivers, but I expect they could be hard to handle in heavy seas."

The *Portland*, lit up from stem to stern, was truly a beautiful sight, but Delia wanted nothing to do with her.

Feeling someone's eyes on her, Delia turned to see a slim dark haired man, in a fur coat and blue vicuna suit, staring boldly at her. As their eyes met, he winked and smiled, and she could see what appeared to be a diamond embedded in one of his large front teeth. A gambler from one of the waterfront saloons, she thought instantly.

Managing a haughty look, she turned away immediately, yet couldn't deny that his attention had momentarily pleased her. It was satisfying to know that at forty-nine a worldly stranger thought her attractive. Out of the corner of her eye she saw him stroll slowly toward the gangplank. As he passed he said in a low voice, "See you on board, darlin'."

Delia turned to face the harbor, taking no chances he might glance back and see her looking after him.

Her vision of the two doomed vessels, and the coffin and schooner symbols formed by the tea leaves, returned to haunt her. In January of last year, just a few days before May died, she had seen a funeral wreath in the girl's cup.

She sighed deeply. When that child died it had been like losing a daughter of their own.

A tall young sailor walked by, his dark hair and big frame reminding Delia of the way Frank must have looked at that age. If only she had been able to give him a child. Of course she was now at the end of her child bearing years, so they never talked about it anymore. She knew she'd disappointed him.

"That's Cap'n Leighton of Rockland," she heard someone say, as an elderly man started up the gangplank, a frown on his face. A few minutes later, he came back down. "You leaving, Cap'n?" he was asked.

"I am," he said. "Don't think this is a fit night to sail. I'm going back to my brother's house in Chelsea." He made his way down the wharf, walking slowly, the way a person does when he is out of health.

His departure made Delia even more apprehensive. She wondered what information a captain might be privy to that passengers were not.

Just then a messenger boy ran up alongside the ship and shouted to one of the porters: "Tell Cap'n Blanchard that Cap'n Dennison of the *Bay State* is calling on the wharf telephone." Delia knew the *Bay State* was the sister ship to the *Portland*.

Soon Captain Blanchard came hurrying down the gangplank. She heard him shouting over the telephone, believing as many seemed to that one had to speak louder when calling a far away place.

"I've had my orders, and I plan to sail," Blanchard told Dennison in a voice almost loud enough to be heard in Portland without the aid of the telephone. Then he added that he'd had a weather report from New York which said the storm was expected to change course.

It seemed to Delia about time for Frank to get back. She looked toward Atlantic Avenue. Could that be Frank getting out of the cab? As the fellow stepped out of the shadows, and under the street light, she saw a shorter, heavier man.

The voices from the lower deck suddenly grew louder, and several people on the wharf pointed toward the top of the gangplank. The ship's tabby cat was walking down it, carrying a kitten in her mouth. She returned to the rocking ship three more times, after which she padded off down the wharf, followed by her four mewing kittens. A fellow who'd been about to board ship turned away and started back toward Atlantic Avenue.

A young man on board called out, "Aren't you sailing with us, Mr. Gott?"

"By Gorry, if the ship's cat won't sail, I won't either," he shouted back.

A murmur of amusement came from the deck. But Delia, who had been raised on a farm, and had seen how animals often knew more than people did about coming storms, felt a chill run down her spine.

She unbuttoned her cape to check her watch, pinned to her suit jacket with a gold fleur-de-lis pin. It read 6:45. The *Portland* would leave at seven.

Delia stood on tiptoe, looking beyond a group of sailors, to see if Frank were coming. No sight of him.

At 6:45 a young man ran up the gangplank.

"There goes Charles, Cap'n Blanchard's oldest boy," she heard one of the longshoremen tell another. "Works right here in Boston."

A few minutes later Charles came walking back down, frowning and shaking his head. Now Delia felt almost sick to her stomach with fear. She prayed Frank wouldn't make it back in time to sail.

As the gangplank was about to be moved, a breathless would-be-passenger sprinted up and landed on deck. Several of those on board gave a cheer, as he shouted, "I made it!"

Then she saw Captain Blanchard on the bridge of the *Portland* and heard him call to the watchman, "If the weather gets too heavy, I'll be back."

Whistles blasted, bells rang, and the *Portland* with her electric lights beaming, moved out into Boston Harbor in a blaze of light.

Although most passengers had gone inside to be out of the cold, a few stood waving from the lower deck.

Now Frank came running down the wharf, and a young couple who appeared to be brother and sister, ran close behind him.

"She sailed, Frank," Delia said, as he stopped beside her.

He nodded. "It doesn't matter, Deal. We'll take the train. What matters is the way I blamed you for forgetting the tickets. When I got back to the house, I remembered what had happened. When I heard the cab coming into the yard, I practically pushed you out the door. You didn't have time to even think, let alone grab your purse. I don't know what got into me."

"It's all right, Frank."

He handed her a large bag in which he'd placed her purse. It would never do for a man to be seen carrying a woman's pocketbook.

"Captain Blanchard, right before he left, told the watchman that if the weather got too heavy, he'd be back," Delia said.

A few more people came running up then, breathlessly bemoaning their missing of the *Portland*.

As Delia and Frank walked back down the wharf, the young couple passed them. "We'll hail a cab for North Station," they heard the fellow tell the girl as they ran by.

"I'm glad we're not going on the *Portland*, Frank," Delia said. "I overheard two merchants talking. They said that the weather bureau in Washington sent a warning wire to shippers this morning. Then I saw Cap'n Leighton of Rockland leave the ship. I heard him say he didn't like the looks of this weather. The ship's cat even brought her kittens off."

Frank shook his head. "Sounds bad." He was quiet for a moment, his forehead creased in a deep frown. "Something's wrong here, Deal. I can't believe the *Portland's* owners, after getting a warning from the weather bureau, would let her leave. I can't figure it out."

Chapter 8

North Station

Snow began to fall, and Delia, afraid of the moisture ruining her hat, paused to put it into the huge bag that held her leather purse. The snow could spot and ruin the looks of both. Frank stopped, too, laying down the three valises.

From a pocket in her fur cape, Delia pulled out a black chiffon scarf. "What kind of a man is Cap'n Blanchard, Frank?"

He looked thoughtful. "Hollis Blanchard is a good man—always does what he believes is right. People say he's a person who thinks a lot of his family, so I know he's grieving right now. I saw in the paper that he just lost a seafaring brother who died east of Hong Kong. With that empty place in his life, I expect he has a need to be with his family now more than ever. I've heard he told the mate he is determined to be home in Yarmouth on Sunday. He plans to have a family dinner with his wife and two of his three children."

Delia, in the midst of wrapping the scarf around her head, to keep her hair dry, turned to stare at Frank. "Are you telling me he might risk the safety of all those aboard because of his own need to be with family?"

"I don't think he would mean to, but sometimes people want things so bad they don't think straight."

As they began walking again, Frank kept turning, trying to see a cab's lanterns through the swirling snow. After a few minutes they heard bells, the kind that in Boston are strung on horses drawing delivery wagons, or tied directly on the wagon thills.

It was a comforting sound to her, bringing her to a solid reality of an everyday life that had nothing to do with the sea or its dangers. The horse, wagon and driver passed by, and soon disappeared into the snowy night.

"Maybe Cap'n Blanchard is like me, Deal," he said after a few minutes. "I wanted to get home real bad. Couldn't admit it wasn't safe to sail.

"I want to see everyone, but Eph the most. I've had some bad work days lately, ornery people to work with. Eph will most likely have some ideas about what I should do. Even if he doesn't, just being with him, talking about old times—the way things used to be—will make me feel better."

They walked on in silence for a few minutes. She pictured Frank's brother Eph, smiling broadly, as he walked out through the snow to help them with the valises. The two brothers had a certain kindness that she seldom saw in other men.

Eph wasn't handsome like Frank. He was of average height—around five feet, eight inches tall, with a stockier build. He had brown hair instead of black, but both had the dark skin and dark eyes.

He moved slowly, never having regained his health since War of the Rebellion days. Although he didn't complain, Delia knew he suffered from rheumatism and heart disease, and got along because of a government pension for soldiers and sailors who could no longer work. But he had a special warmth, which she'd felt the first time she met him.

"Eph's a good person to be with," she said.

"Aye. It's the sea that binds us, Deal. Like our brothers Ozias and Mazina, and our father before us, Eph and I became sailors. When we're together, we go back over those days, and what we went through. We start talking about the past, and then after awhile, we work into the present.

"There are certain things he wants to talk about and he always asks me to tell about being captured by two of the Confederate raiders, the *Alabama* and the *Tallahassee*. That happened when I sailed on merchant schooners carrying lumber, while soldiers fought the War of the Rebellion on land."

Her tragic vision of the young man at the wheel of the little schooner, and the sounds of the screams coming from the great mist-covered liner returned with such force, that she found it hard to concentrate on Frank's story.

"...All of us aboard that first captured lumber schooner thought the *Alabama* another sailing ship...but she came too fast. I saw a steam engine brought up through the deck. Our schooner...ransacked and burned...taken with forty four prisoners, from their last three vessels. We were put aboard an old brigantine...left us off not too far from our homes, Monhegan for me ... stayed a few days with my father's people...sailed back to Pemaquid Harbor with the fellow who went to get the mail.

"Then more bad luck...next time out, the schooner I sailed on...taken by the *Tallahassee*. Once again, the vessel I'd been on...burned. This time we were ordered onto an English ship and put ashore in Nova Scotia."

When the familiar name of Nova Scotia came into her consciousness, she managed, with effort, to temporarily put aside the sights and sounds of her vision and listen to Frank.

"You were right across from where I lived," Delia said, "on the other side of the Bay of Fundy. During the last part of the war, St. John was crowded with Confederates. I heard that if one counted the Rebel refugees in all the ports, there would be about fifteen thousand in Canada.

"My father wouldn't let me go into town unless two of my older brothers went with me, one on either side. We knew some of the men had escaped from prison camps along the Great Lakes. Others had run the Union blockade of Southern ports or stolen through battle lines. Some of them got together and made raids across the border into Maine and Vermont. 'Desperate men,' my father called them. But they all seemed very pleasant and mannerly to me."

Frank looked amused. "What young man wouldn't be pleasant and mannerly to a pretty girl like you?" He looked back over his shoulder to see if the lights from a cab could be seen through the falling snow. No luck.

Delia felt a rising nervousness. What if a cab didn't come? Frank didn't seem worried, though...just went on talking in a calm voice.

"When I talk to Eph about happenings at sea, I tell all the details, and him having been a sailor, he understands. There's a comfort in that."

I'm here, Frank, she wanted to say. Why isn't it a comfort to talk to me? Then she thought about how it was when she got together with her brother George.

The two of them would laugh about things in the past, things that happened when they were children living in St. John. She would try to explain to Frank why they were laughing, but he didn't understand. It was a part of her life he couldn't share because he hadn't been there.

The temperature had fallen so swiftly that her hands and feet began aching with the cold.

Frank turned to look back over his shoulder. "I think I hear a cab coming."

She heard the muffled sound of horse's hooves on the snow covered street, then saw two misty lights from carriage lanterns. It brought back the memory of the misty light surrounding her vision of the great liner breaking apart, and of the young man at the wheel of the little schooner that disappeared into the sea.

"Over here!" Frank shouted, and the horse and carriage appeared out of a curtain of snow. "North Station!" he ordered, before stashing the valises in the back and helping Delia up into the cab.

"Nasty night," the driver said, then shouted, "Giddap!" to the horse. "This is my last run. It's getting worse all the time."

Delia clasped her hands tightly together inside her muff and turned toward Frank. "Maybe we should go on home now. That would be the safest place."

Frank laughed. "Nothing is going to bother a great train, Deal."

When the cab pulled up to the station, the snow was blowing harder. After lifting the three valises from the back and paying the cabby, Frank helped Delia down from the cab and they walked, heads down, in the direction of the main door. She held onto the sleeve of his coat so they wouldn't get separated. Once inside, Delia immediately took off her soaking wet scarf, then after both had shaken off as much snow as possible, they turned to the right and entered the crowded waiting room.

Frank found a place for them to sit, and put their valises on the long seat, to show an area big enough for two people was taken. While he went to buy the tickets, she stepped to a nearby counter to order two cups of hot chocolate. Right now they needed to get warm. If they were hungry later, they could buy sandwiches aboard the train.

She listened to the eerie sound of the wind, as it began to whine around the station, and murmured thanks that they weren't at sea.

When Frank came back from the ticket counter, he looked frustrated. "No more seats left on the next train. They said the Charles River is threatening to flood its banks. If that happens, the later trains won't be able to cross it. I wouldn't be surprised if we were here all night."

Delia sighed. "We'll be so tired, Frank, sitting up all those hours. Why don't we go home, get a good night's rest, then get a fresh start in the morning?"

"Not possible. The fellow at the ticket desk said all the cabs and hacks have left."

Frank was restless, and stepped outside to see if the weather showed any signs of improving. He returned rather quickly, blowing on his hands to warm them. "No sign of the heavy weather letting up, Deal. The snow is blowing into both ends of the train sheds. There's a gang of shovelers out there trying to keep the tracks clear. I imagine some of the trains will get snowed up before they ever get here."

"That could happen," Delia said, "as heavy as it's falling. She pulled her damp hat from the bag, placed it on an old newspaper, and pushed it under her chair. Two men sitting behind them were talking about what they had seen at the Mechanic's Fair. She noticed several families with young children. She supposed they had been visiting grandparents over the Thanksgiving holiday, and were now headed home.

Directly across from them, a curly haired little fellow in a sailor dress with anchors on the collar, his chubby legs encased in scarlet stockings, smiled shyly at them from the safety of his father's lap. The weary looking young mother held a crying infant. Several strands of her pale blonde hair had escaped her hair pins and hung limply at the sides of her thin face.

The young father, who had the brown, spare look of a sailor, held his left arm around his restless toddler, and extending his right hand, leaned across toward Frank. "Joshua Adams here," he said.

Delia watched as her husband grasped it.

"Frank Stevens."

"Pleased to meet you, Mr. Stevens. This is my wife, Mary, holding our three-month old daughter, Faith, and this two-year old rascal on my lap is Jonathan."

"I'd like you to meet my wife, Delia," Frank said, and the two women exchanged smiles.

Joshua looked across at Frank. "Sure hate to be marooned here tonight, but it's better than being on the water."

"My thoughts exactly!"

The baby's eyes were closing, and she appeared to be drifting off. For a while everyone spoke in low voices, then stopped talking altogether, hoping she would go to sleep and let her mother get some rest.

Frank got up and walked around the waiting room to stretch his legs. He bought a "Boston Post," read for only a short while, then dozed off. After a few minutes, his face took on a worried look. He began saying something in his sleep, and she leaned close to hear what it was.

"Don't cry, Cretia," he said. "I didn't mean those things I said."

A chill went through Delia. Cretia was his first wife. How strange that after all these years he had them confused.

His lips were moving again. "I don't mind that you didn't fix supper or iron my shirt. You just rest—like the doctor said."

Delia knew that Lucretia had died at 21 of two dreadful diseases, scrofula and phthisis, after they'd been married only a year and a half. With scrofula, one had the swelling of the glands, and the breaking out in sores. With phthisis, which was consumption of the lungs, came a terrible, strangling cough.

Frank seemed to be reliving the time when she first started feeling poorly, when he didn't yet understand how seriously ill she was becoming. He must have been cross with her, and had never forgiven himself for it.

Eph had told Delia that after Lucretia's death, Frank had locked up his house, broken hearted, and gotten as far away from Boston as he could. He'd sailed from Boston on an English ship, replacing a sailor who'd died at sea. Upon reaching the British Isles, he'd signed on to a brig collier bound for Taganrog on the Black Sea, then, after the return to England, had been cast ashore on Goodwin Sands in the English Channel. He'd worked his way home.

"It's all right, dear," she said, patting his hand to awaken him.

His eyes had a haunted look when he opened them, but after a moment he smiled at her with an expression of relief. "I was having a bad dream."

Delia had discovered in her early days of marriage that although he never spoke of his first wife, she was not forgotten. One day she decided to surprise him by cleaning out the drawers of the bureau and lining them with fresh newspaper. She could hardly believe it when under the paper in his top drawer she found a small daguerreotype of Lucretia.

On his return from the wharf that evening, she announced, "I cleaned out all the bureau drawers today and lined them with fresh newspaper." They were standing in the bedroom when she said it.

A startled look came into his eyes, and he whirled around to open his top drawer. There, lying on his best shirt, was the likeness of his young first wife, now in a beautiful gold frame.

As he turned to face Delia, the daguerreotype in his hand, and tears in his eyes, she said, "We mustn't ever forget those we've loved Frank."

He had leaned forward and kissed her. It had done a lot for their marriage.

She was feeling tired, but as she closed her eyes, the thought came to her that she mustn't go to sleep yet. This was the time to tell her husband about the tea leaves and the vision.

"Frank," she whispered, "there are a couple of things you should know." There was a tremor in her voice that must have warned him this would be no ordinary conversation, because he turned his head quickly toward her, his eyes alert and wary.

"You remember that before we left the house I read the tea leaves?"

He nodded, watching her closely. "What did you see?"

Delia repeated the story.

"Good Lord!" he said as she finished. He reached over to take her hand. "If we could sort out what schooner you saw, we'd know the person at the wheel. But that doesn't seem possible. I don't believe any of our people were among those poor souls on the steamer."

"I don't think so."

"Would any of your nephews in St. John be out in their schooners?"

She took a deep, shaky breath. "Most likely."

"But you don't know for certain."

"No."

"I've been thinking of my nephews in Pemaquid Harbor. Eph's, Euda's, and Cretia's boys make their living off the water, lobstering or going on short hauls, but none are that far from home. Only Zena's boys are at sea." He waited a moment, collecting his emotions. "Lem is down around the Caribbean or South Atlantic, but the other two are most likely out in this gale. We know from Lawrence's and Percy's letters that the *Robert A.* is bound for Salem, and the *Addie E.*, New York."

"Frank, when I saw that schooner in my vision, I thought right away the young man at the wheel might be Lawrence. Remember the last time we saw in the shipping news that the *Addie E.* had come into Boston

Harbor? Percy was still mate, then, and Lawrence and Myrtie Belle newly married. When we went to meet them, Lawrence seemed to concentrate on his bride so completely, you later joked that you wondered if he could keep his wits about him at sea. I had wondered, quite seriously, myself, when he started out in the wrong direction for the restaurant where we always eat.

"At the table, it was Percy who kept the conversation going. I don't remember much of what was said. All that sticks in my mind, is when his haddock was served, he said he wished he could trade it for a fish called red snapper."

"Want drink, Papa," the little boy across the aisle said in a piping voice.

The father, stood up and carried the child to where there were paper cups and ice water.

"Good!" the child said as he took a swallow from the cup. At that moment the wind outside shrieked wildly, frightening the little boy, who cried out as he spilled the cold water down the front of his dress.

Others looked on sympathetically as the mother tucked a dry cloth inside of the sobbing child's undershirt.

Frank seemed unaware of what was going on, staring glumly off into the distance. Finally he said, "We're helpless, hon. We can't do a thing about what's going to happen at sea." He stood up. "I imagine the heavy weather will reach Maine in a few hours, and Eph, thinking we're at sea, will worry about us. I'm going to send him a wire."

"Good idea." As she watched him walk to the office, she was aware of the wind moaning along the tracks ... screaming about the building.

He returned almost immediately. "Telegraph lines are down, Deal. We're completely cut off."

Chapter 9

Lost on Land

Zena

Icy snow beat against the house, and the wind screamed about the eaves, waking all who slept. The grandfather clock, in the little front hall, struck three times.

For Zena, Joe, and Josie, haunted by visions of mast-high waves and ice-covered schooners, going back to sleep was impossible. The wind hurled snow down the chimney; the fire on the hearth sputtered; threatened to go out; and Joe had to coax it back with thin curls of shaved wood. Water seeped in around the window glass, and drops from the ceiling above the windows made small pools on the floor.

Josie, in a long white nightgown with ribbon trim around the neck and sleeves, mopped up the water. Zena, in her heavy white flannel nightgown, and the black and lilac slippers, Josie had crocheted for her last Christmas, placed pots and pans beneath the leaks, then found towels and rags to lay on the window sills. Joe, who had come home at dusk, singing at the top of his voice and unaware of the coming storm sat on the deacon's bench, shaving thin curls from a stick of firewood. He had pulled on patched and faded denim work pants over his long-handled red underwear.

He stopped working with the fire for a few minutes, while he looked for their clothes rack, which he placed in front of the hearth, so they could hang the wet rags and towels on its rungs. Drops of water from the ceiling above the windows plinked noisily into the pots and pans on the floor.

From time to time Joe pressed a hand against his forehead, as one does when one has a headache.

Whenever there came a few minutes between tasks, Zena sat down, opened the big family Bible to Psalms, and read appropriate verses aloud:

"'In thee, O Lord, do I put my trust....

"Let my prayer come before thee: incline thine ear unto my cry....

"Thou rulest the raging of the sea: when the waves thereof arise, thou stillest them.'"

"Always speak aloud the word of the Lord, Josie," she counseled. "It's a mighty protection against evil."

But Josie was too distracted to listen. She continually ran up from the kitchen to the second floor, then down again, changing rags on the window sills, making sure to empty the water pans before they overflowed.

"Sit and rest for a bit, child," Zena said. "Do some sewing for awhile." Josie had been seated for just a few minutes, hemming the skirt of her new mulberry colored suit, when her head drooped forward, and her long auburn lashes rested on her cheeks.

Outside, the wind continued to shriek and groan. Then along Wawenock Ridge came a heavy, rushing sound like that of a freight train. When it struck with a frightful roar, the house shook on its foundation.

The ship in the bottle, that Percy had brought back from New Orleans, teetered at the edge of the mantel, but Zena caught it.

Joe, a startled look on his face, rose half way off the deacon's bench. "Never heard the like, never! Came out of nowhere! Hit us, too!"

"What was that!?" Josie cried. She was on her feet now, her eyes wide open.

"A tornado?" Zena said. "I think that's the way they sound."

Josie shook from fright. "A tornado! I've never heard of them around here. I thought they just happened in the West." She bent over to pick up the partly hemmed skirt that had fallen to the floor.

"God help the boys on a night like this!" Joe said in a husky voice. His face had turned pale, and he began pacing back and forth across the kitchen floor, wringing his hands. "We're poor miserable critters," he muttered, "just poor miserable critters."

An evil wind shrieked and threw things against the house. Zena looked down at her Bible again, hunting for the needed verses. God's word would help her through whatever happened. She had begun her study of it as a young girl, and gradually she, like her mother before her, had grown to depend on it. Now the verses were her guide and comforter.

Zena's back ached from the bending to pick up heavy pots and pans, and empty them. To lie down for just a few minutes would help. She headed for the bedroom. Before stretching out on the bed, however, Zena knelt to say her prayers. "God hears better when you're on your knees," her mother used to say. She took off the crocheted slippers, damp from stepping in puddles on the floor, and put them on a small braided rug by her side of the bed. Branches of the pine and hemlock trees scraped against the house.

Through the slightly open bedroom door she saw Joe pace back and forth across the kitchen floor, wringing his hands. Because of the storm's noise she couldn't hear what he said, but could read his lips. He repeated over and over, "God help the boys on a night like this."

And Myrtie Belle, Zena thought. She wondered if the girl's father, Thomas Jefferson Brown, was wearing a path in his kitchen floor in Rockland. She suspected that he was. After a few minutes, she got up and went back into the kitchen.

She sat on the deacon's bench and, looking at Joe, patted the empty place beside her, for him to sit down. "Rest now, dear. You'll wear yourself out."

Still wringing his hands, he sat beside her. After a few minutes, he asked, "Where'd I put that tobacco I bought in Scotty?" Zena found the three plugs on the sideboard. He took out his pocket knife and began shaving one into the bowl of his corncob pipe. He smoked for awhile, then his head began to nod. When the pipe hung loosely from his mouth, she took it. "Go to bed, Joe," she said. "I'll be along in a minute."

Zena looked across at Josie and saw that her eyes were closed. She took the finished skirt from her lap and laid it carefully in the bottom drawer of the sideboard. "Go on upstairs now, child," she said.

When Josie had left, Zena walked slowly into the bedroom. Joe was snoring loudly. Once again she got on her knees, and prayed that the Lord would watch over the boys.

She climbed into bed, but didn't sleep. The noise outside got louder. The wind rattled the windows until she feared they would break.

The storm must be doing great damage along their shore, perhaps destroying their two small businesses—the weir and the brickyard. The rocky farmland didn't earn enough to live on. Most likely the weir, just beyond the river banks, was wrecked. She pictured churning water washing away the brush between the weir's rough cut alder posts, tearing the nets, then breaking off the posts themselves. Perhaps the wind had torn down the shacks where alewives were hung and smoked, as well as the high shed roofing above the brickyard kiln.

Maybe everything was gone, but it didn't really matter. None of it did. Nothing was of any importance except the boys. Zena was afraid to even imagine what it was like at sea...what their boys might be going through. The only way she knew to protect them was through ceaseless prayer.

Joe turned restlessly, and pulled at the comforter.

Zena could hear big drops of water plunking into a pan near the window, and got up to empty it. The water was coming in so steadily that the pots and pans on both floors had to be emptied frequently. The cloths on the window sills were soaking wet and needed to be exchanged for the dry ones hanging on the rack in front of the kitchen hearth. She was up and down the rest of the night and, while up, jammed more wood into the stove, and lay another stick or two in the fireplaces. She was conscious of the grandfather clock striking the hours and half hours, providing some order in a world gone mad.

Toward time for the sun to rise, she once again emptied pots and pans, exchanged wet cloths for drier ones, then made her way to bed, and fell asleep from exhaustion. Neither she nor Joe opened their eyes until the grandfather clock called out eight times.

Joe sat up in bed and looked around. A bit of light in the room shone from the fireplace embers. "Can't be morning," he said. "Didn't hear the cock crow." He got out of bed in his long handled red underwear, and walked stiffly to the nearest bedroom window. "Dad gum floor's wet," he said, as he pulled up the olive green shade and looked outside. "Black as night out there." Then they heard the scream of an angry wind as it smashed things against the house. "Oh God, Zena—this storm—the worst ever! Them boys—think they've got a chance?"

Zena, dark circles under her eyes, spoke in a voice that could barely be heard. "Don't know...have to keep praying."

They heard Josie run down the steps from her bedroom. In a few seconds she was standing in the open doorway, dressed in her "Gibson Girl" shirtwaist and skirt, her hair neatly pulled back with a blue moire ribbon tied in a bow. "You two get dressed while I heat up the beans and brown bread," she said with a smile. "Then I'll tell you my good news!"

Zena and Joe looked at each other in amazement. "Good news?"

"Well, hurry and get dressed!" Josie had suddenly become the parent and they the children.

In a few minutes they appeared in the kitchen, fully dressed. Josie, who had donned a flowered apron, smiled in spite of the roaring and howling of the wind.

"I had a wonderful dream," she said, her eyes glowing. "It was summer time, and all of our family and relatives, including the Stevenses and Fitches, were together—having a lawn party. Why, there must have been half a hundred of us. I remember a big cake with white frosting. Lemmie and Lawrence, and Bernard and Ralph had their arms about each others' shoulders, and they were singing 'Row, Row, Row Your Boat;' and the aunts and uncles were all laughing and talking. Then the dream slowly faded. I know it was a glimpse into the future—a glimpse into a happy future."

Joe looked at Zena with an expression of relief.

"Did you see Percy, Josie?" Zena asked.

Josie stopped ladling the reheated beans from the black iron spider. "The dream came and went so quickly I didn't have time to sort everyone out, but he must have been. The whole family was there—and we were all so happy!" She filled her mother's cup with tea and her father's with coffee.

The hot coffee, tasty reheated beans, and the toasted and buttered brown bread, along with Josie's dream, had gave Joe courage. "Lawrence and Percy are safe in port this morning, and Lem, too," he announced in a voice so tense that it cracked. "Don't know if he's in the Caribbean or the South Atlantic—but he's safe!"

"You're right, Father," Josie said, "I know you are."

Zena finished her tea and got up to get her Bible, but before sitting down, pulled the rocker away from the window, away from the icy drafts. She opened the Bible to Psalms, but too tired to read, stayed with her eyes closed and said her endless prayers. She heard the clink of the cups, saucers and plates, as Josie collected the dishes from the table, then lost track of time for awhile. She came partly awake with the rhythmic swish of Josie's broom back and forth across wide pine floor boards.

Through half open eyes Zena saw Joe add more wood to the fire as Josie emptied the pots and pans. The girl was walking past the windows at the back of the kitchen, picking up the sopping wet rags along the sills, when suddenly she shouted, "Look! Look outside! It's getting light! The storm is ending!"

"Praise the Lord!" Zena cried.

Joe stood up and started toward the back windows so fast he caught his foot in the rack and almost fell. As father and daughter looked down over the fields and woods, and river, Josie shook her head in wonder at what she saw. "Looks like a different world out there. Branches are broken off the trees, and our beautiful river looks rough and wild."

"See how them two big spruces are uprooted—pulled right up out of the earth," Joe said, awe in his voice.

"Look out front here!" Zena cried. "The telegraph poles are broken off. Wires are under the drifts. We wouldn't be able to get any messages in case...."

"Zena!" Joe said crossly. "Didn't you understand what Josie told us? Everyone is fine!"

Now that the roaring of the storm had ended, they could hear the distant mooing of the cows whose bags were filled to bursting.

"Poor critters," Joe said. "I better get out to the barn. You come along and help me, Josie."

They put on their fearnoughts, high boots, thick gloves and knitted hats. Zena wrapped wool mufflers over their mouths and noses so that just their eyes showed. Joe pushed open the back door and, carrying milk pails, they walked across an icy film on top of the snow.

Zena, as she watched them through the window, had all she could do to keep herself from running to the door and calling, "Come back, come back!" Why am I so afraid for them? she asked herself. They're only going to the barn. I'm getting to be a foolish old woman. However, as she washed and dried the dishes, and looked out at the devastation down Wawenock Ridge, then began tidying up the bedroom, the feeling persisted.

When she bent to put dry rags on a window sill, a heavy wind struck the glass in front of her face—so hard that she cried out. As she looked outside, the sun vanished, and all she could see was darkness. The storm was back. "Oh Lord! Oh Lord!" That short spell of light and quiet must have been the eye of the storm passing over.

The wind screamed even louder than before, and something in the wildness of it made her shiver. "Oh Lord! I've been praying I wouldn't lose my boys at sea. Now I may lose my husband and my only daughter right here on our own land."

She quickly lit all the kerosene lamps, and hurried to place one in each window. The light might guide them to the house. In the darkness and swirling snow, they would have no sense of direction.

Zena threw on her cloak, and pulled on Joe's old stocking cap. She opened the door—and the wind pinned her to it. Although she tried to shout, "Josie! Joe!" the freezing wind took her breath away.

Icy snow hit her face with such force that it felt like sharp little rocks. She drew in her breath, then let out a long "Hello-o-o," but the howling storm swallowed the sound. All she could see before her was a curtain of snow. Then, for a second, a crosswise current pushed the falling snow upward, and Zena saw Joe and Josie—but they were going the wrong way—toward the woods and river. Abruptly the storm closed in again and they disappeared from sight.

She wanted to run out into the storm to get them, but knew that she, too, might get lost. Then they would have no chance at all. "Oh Lord," she cried, "tell me what I can do to save them. What? The snowfall is so heavy they won't see the lamplight."

Her mind went empty, and a voice in her head said, "Get the gun."

She raced to get Joe's shotgun, braced herself against the door and fired toward the sky. Pulling her muffler up over her nose so she didn't have to breathe the freezing air, she fired at regular intervals.

The ammunition began to run low, and a cold fear lurked inside of her. They would freeze to death if they stayed out much longer. She fired at longer intervals now, and between shots, shouted. Then above the roar and scream of the wind she heard an answering cry. She reached out to touch a solid figure, and in a moment all three were inside.

Safe in the kitchen, with the door shut, they were suddenly in a quiet refuge, away from the piercing shriek of the wind and sharp bite of the cold. They stood in a tight three-person circle, their arms around each other, momentarily wordless in their gratitude.

Then Joe took a deep breath, and his voice shook as he spoke. "Fierce out there, Zena. Couldn't stand alone—had to lean against each other. Couldn't see but a few inches ahead. Had no idea which way we were going. Then, a miracle. We heard your shots, and we followed the sounds."

Josie began sobbing. "We could have frozen to death out there, just a little way from the house."

"Is there any feeling in your feet?" Zena asked.

"No," Josie said. "They're like blocks of ice."

"You both sit down and I'll pull your boots off," Zena directed. Their fingers would be too stiff to do it for themselves. Under Joe's side of the bed she found him an old pair of sheep-skin slippers, for wearing inside rubber boots; gave her now dry ones to Josie, then laid newspapers over the wet floor.

"We've got to walk, Josie," Joe said. "We can't stop till the feeling comes back in our feet."

Zena knew that although as terrible as the storm was on land, it would be worse at sea, but she couldn't allow herself to think about that now—just about Joe and Josie. She prayed they wouldn't lose their toes.

From a drawer in the sideboard, she pulled a folded piece of red flannel. To warm it, she hung it over a chair in front of the opened oven door. From a brown and tan crock in the cellarway she spooned hardened goose grease into a small pan and put it on the back of the woodstove to let it turn to liquid.

"I'm getting a bad headache and a sore throat," Josie said.

Joe, whose face looked feverish, coughed several times.

Zena hurried into the summer kitchen for another bottle of the dried bark of white willow. She'd given Mr. Owen one, but had at least a dozen left. She measured half a teaspoonful of the medicine into each of two cups. This should help relieve the fever, sore throat, and headache, she said to herself. She mixed in water from the iron tea kettle and added licorice, also a good medicine for colds, but mainly to offset the bitterness of the willow bark.

When Joe and Josie felt their blood circulating freely again, they counted themselves lucky neither had any dead spots in their feet, legs, hands or face.

They sat and drank their hot willow tea, but Josie still felt cold.

She shivered and wrapped her arms around herself. "I wonder if I'll ever feel warm again."

Zena's forehead creased in a worried frown. "You know how easily you get pneumonia, Josie. Rub some of this goose grease on your chest, then cover it with this piece of warmed flannel. Tonight I want you to stay in the birthing room, off your father's and my bedroom, where I can look in on you."

When Josie left the kitchen, Joe got up, took a cup off a shelf and filled it from the teapot kept at the back of the stove. He stirred in sugar, then carried it carefully across the kitchen to where Zena sat in her rocking chair. A tender light shown in his blue eye as he bent to place the cup in her hands.

"You saved us, Zena," he said. "If it wasn't for them gun shots, we'd never have made it."

She looked up at him through a mist of tears.

Chapter 10

The Storm at Pemaquid Harbor

Hattie Belle

"The gale's begun!" Captain Davis called out as he rapped on Hattie Belle's bedroom door. "Everybody downstairs."

"All right, Papa," Hattie Belle said, suddenly awake. From outside came the roar of the wind.

"Is this really necessary, Will?" she heard Mary ask.

"I've got a bad feeling about this storm. Can't tell what might happen here along the water. It'll be safer if we're all together."

"Take your flatiron with you, then," Mary said. "It'll need reheating before we come back up."

With the aid of light from kerosene lamps, they found their way down the dark hall, then the back stairs. In the kitchen, each one placed a flatiron, which had been used as a bed warmer, on the hottest part of the woodstove. But by this time, the fire had died way back.

Hattie Belle and Captain Davis hurried to a kitchen window, and watched tensely as moonlight revealed the usually calm harbor churned into great waves, and tossing about vessels, as if they were no more than the paper boats of children.

A strong, icy wind rattled the damper on the stove pipe, a cold and lonely sound. The fire had been banked with hardwood, so all Mary had to do to bring it back, was to put another stick of oak on the coals. Uninterested in the ships, she took her fancy work from the bottom drawer in the sideboard, pulled a chair near the woodstove, and went on with her everlasting tatting.

"Look at the *Chamberlain*," Hattie Belle cried. "She's broken loose from her moorings. She's going to run into that coal barge. Oh!... She clapped both hands over her eyes, then when she dared to look, sighed with relief. "They missed each other, thank heaven."

"By gorry, look how that schooner pitches in those heavy seas," Captain Davis said. They stared out the window, but soon dark clouds covered the face of the moon, and erased their view.

Captain Davis continued to watch through his spyglass until the clouds parted for a few seconds. "There's the *Chamberlain*, again, headed out to sea!" he cried. The darkness crowded in again, but Hattie Belle noticed that her father stood taller than he had in a long while, and a youthful set graced his lined face.

She knew that, in spite of the danger, he wished he were on that schooner, salt spray stinging his face, the sea washing over the deck.

Mary, almost finished with another of her knotted lace creations, looked up from her work. "Aren't you glad to be a farmer now, Will, done with that terrible seafaring life?"

He turned slowly, with a look of disbelief, then faced the window again. "How little you know me," he muttered.

After a few minutes, Mary held up the decorative piece to be admired. "These will look nice on the backs of overstuffed furniture, and at the same time save them from being stained by men's hair oil. Do you like this, Will?" She looked toward Captain Davis, who still stood in front of the window, staring out into the harbor. He hadn't heard a word.

She raised her voice. "I keep telling you, Will, that we should move farther back from the sea. In Damariscotta Mills, where I grew up, storms were never this bad."

"Storms were never this bad anywhere!" he said sharply. The subject of leaving this place by the harbor, with the North Atlantic in the distance, had become a sore one between them.

"I hate the sea!" Mary said. "It's so vicious!"

A shocked look crossed Captain Davis's face, but he said nothing.

"It's becoming a terribly cold night," Mary said, "—down here along the water."

Hattie Belle turned away from the window. She added another stick of wood to the fire, and smoothed out the big padded squares, cut from an old quilt, which enabled people to carry a hot iron without being burnt.

Captain Davis sat down in his rocker, lit his briar pipe, and continued to stare out into the darkness, his spyglass in his lap.

When thunder sounded and streaks of lightning cut their way through the darkness, Hattie Belle ran back to the window and caught another glimpse of high froth tipped waves in the blackened water. Scenes from her nightmare about the *Scorpion* and Lemmie ran through her head.

Mary pulled out the bottom drawer of the sideboard, and carefully laid the antimacassar on top of the others. Christmas was less than a month away. "We've been up for two hours, worrying," she said, "but the storm goes on. We might as well try to get some rest."

Captain Davis got to his feet. "I reckon sitting here isn't going to do anyone any good." Shaking his head at the shrieks of the wind as it hurled rough shore sand against the house, he lifted a stove lid and knocked the ashes from his pipe into the fire.

They each picked up a hot flatiron and wrapped it in a quilted square. Captain Davis and Hattie Belle picked up a kerosene lamp as well, and all headed toward the back stairway. A loud crash of thunder echoed through the house, and he stopped abruptly. "Pity the poor sailors on a night like this!"

When Mary opened the door, the lamplight flickered against the wainscot panelling, and freezing cold air from the unheated second floor rushed down to meet them.

In her room, Hattie Belle reached under the quilts, ran her hot flatiron across the flannel sheets on her bed, then placed it, re-wrapped, near where her feet would be. Outside, broken branches struck the house like a succession of staccato notes. Great waves crashed against the rocks, and the wind moaned.

Hattie Belle's mother, a music teacher, had taught her to hear songs in the sound of wind, the cry of gulls, and the lapping of water against rocks, but tonight nature played a discordant piece.

Her spirits low, she doubted Lemmie would return. Some people weren't meant for happiness. She pulled tortoise shell pins from the coil at the nape of her neck, and her hair fell around her like a mantle, long enough to sit on, just as her mother's had.

Hattie Belle had been eight when her mother's coughing spells began. A particular morning stood out in her mind. Her mother was sitting in a chair by a kitchen window, a red shawl around her shoulders; her sister May stood at the work table rolling out pie crust, a smudge of flour on her forehead.

A tintype, taken that year, helped Hattie Belle to visualize herself as she looked that day—a thin child with big blue-grey eyes and blonde pigtails. She watched from a space of 17 years as the scene played itself out in her mind.

"Let's walk down to the shore, Mama," the little girl begged as she pulled on her mother's arm. "Let's have a tea party on the rocks, the way we used to. Please, Mama, please!"

"Not today, Hattie Belle. We'll do it when I feel better."

"B-but you said that yesterday, Mama," the little girl said, her eyes filling with tears.

"Don't cry, Hattie Belle," May said. "If you are a good girl and let Mama rest, when I get done here I'll play a game of checkers with you. Look, I'm making a special little tart just for you."

The wind shrieked around the house—cursing everything in its path. How much her life had been like that—getting hurt again and again.

She thought of the afternoon when all her mother's brothers and sisters, who lived anywhere near, came with their wives or husbands. Nanny was already there, also the doctor, in the bedroom across the hall from the kitchen...tending to her mother.

Hattie Belle remembered that as a child, she had loved family get-togethers, but that day had seemed different from the others. Everyone was so quiet—almost whispering. She overheard the words "galloping consumption."

The doctor came out of Mama's room for a moment to get a cup of coffee and a molasses cookie, but Papa didn't come at all. "He says he can't eat," the doctor said, and the grown-ups nodded. It seemed strange that he didn't want anything because Papa was a hearty eater.

Uncle Louis got a piece of penuche from a fancy dish on the sideboard, carried it in his calloused fingers to put in her hand.

"Oh my goodness," Hattie Belle said, smiling, "but I didn't eat my parsnips, Uncle Louis. Do you think Mama will mind?"

He wiped a hand across his eyes. "No, honey, she won't mind."

There was the lovely smell of lavender water, and she turned to see Nanny Lewis come into the room and whisper something to Uncle George.

"It's our turn to see Gussie now," he said to Aunt Jennie.

Hattie Belle ate the big piece of brown sugar candy slowly, to make it last. Her grandmother sat down in her son's empty chair and reached over to stroke one of the little girl's blonde pigtails. "Do you realize how ill your mother is?" she asked softly.

"I know, Nanny. That is why May and I are doing all the work...so she can rest and the doctor can help her get better."

"But Hattie Belle...."

"I dry all the dishes and set the table. I feed the hens, too. When Mama gets better we're going to walk down to the shore and have a tea party on the rocks. She promised!"

When it was Hattie Belle's bedtime, she skipped from one to the other of her aunts and uncles for a hug and a kiss. Her father and grandmother were still with her mother. Suddenly there was a strangling cough from the bedroom. "I want to see Mama," she said, alarmed at the sound.

"The doctor is with her now," Aunt Jennie said. "Let's go upstairs and see what we can find on your pillow."

Hattie Belle raced up the steps. "Oh, a little autograph book," she squealed. "Just what I wanted. May I hold it while I go to sleep?"

"Of course you may."

As her aunt tucked her in, the little girl looked up happily and said, "Today is almost like Christmas, isn't it Aunt Jennie?"

Through the mists of sleep she heard her grandmother's voice, and smelled the faint suggestion of lavender. "Wake up, child. Quickly! Your mother is calling for you." She grasped Hattie Belle's hand, and hurried the little girl through the dark hall and down the back stairs.

Hattie Belle was surprised to see all the aunts and uncles in her mother's bedroom. Her Uncle George was reading from the Bible: "Yea though I walk through the valley of the shadow...."

Her mother's eyes turned to look at Hattie Belle. "Be a good girl," she whispered through parched lips, "and always obey your father."

"Come now," her grandmother whispered in her ear, and half pulled the little girl back upstairs, back down the hall, into her bedroom.

"Something is wrong, Nanny," Hattie Belle said tremulously. "The doctor isn't making Mama get better."

"Oh child—child," her grandmother said, "doctors can't do everything. Now, Hattie Belle, you stay in bed and don't get up until I come for you." With that, she hurried out of the room, and closed the door behind her.

Hattie Belle found the little autograph book between the sheets and held its cover against her cheek. "I'll show you to Mama in the morning," she said. "I'll say, 'Mama, you can be the first one to write in my new book.' That will make her so happy." After awhile she closed her eyes.

She awoke to find May's arms around her, and May sobbing. "Oh, Hattie Belle, what will we do?...what will we do? Mama's gone now, and Papa is lying face down on the ground outside her window."

Everything remained so clear in her mind that it seemed hard to believe it had all happened 17 years ago. Since that night, nothing had been the same. Her pillow was wet with tears she hadn't realized she'd shed.

The wind kept throwing broken branches against the house, a lonely, hopeless sound. She reached one hand outside the covers, and felt across the icy cold surface of her bedside stand for the silver box with the gold plush dome. Yes, there it was, holding in its silken interior the exquisite gold ring with its four rubies, the promise of marriage to Lemmie, and a new life.

She liked to pretend it would happen, but everyone she had ever loved had left her: her mother, her sister May; Frank, to whom she'd given her heart; even her father, who had left her for nine months of each year with a stepmother who recited all of his daughter's childish shortcomings when he came home from sea.

If the *Scorpion* failed to come into New York, Hattie Belle planned go to live in East Boston with Aunt Mary, her father's sister, who had often begged her to come. I'll miss Papa, she thought, and this old house where so many memories of Mama still linger, but I can teach school there as well as here, and I won't be under the same roof with my stepmother.

The scenes from her nightmare had now become a firm reality in her mind. She visualized again and again the vessel caught in the trough of the sea with a broken steering wheel, great waves sweeping over the deck. It seemed unlikely Lemmie would survive the hurricane. Still, two and a half years ago, in April of '96, when he'd been caught in a week of storms, with his schooner *Sheepscot* in a sinking condition, he'd survived—through the grace of God.

Will you come back to me again, Lemmie? she asked as thunder rolled ominously though the sky and wind rattled the bedroom window. She remembered the delicious excitement she'd felt in his arms. Would he return; would things be as they used to be? If he did return, things would not be exactly the way they were. She'd learned long ago that nothing is ever just as it used to be.

Her thoughts went back to a long ago spring, the first one after Mama's death. She'd held May's hand as they walked along the side of the muddy road toward the post office. As they passed the house where Nanny Lewis lived, May said, "Look there in the yard, Hattie Belle—the first robin! Make a wish on him and it will come true."

She made her wish, dropped May's hand, and raced back to the house. When it came true everything would be as it used to be. She'd hear the tick of the metronome keeping time, as one of the music students played Mama's favorite piece, "Beautiful Dreamer," on the melodeon.

She reached home, ran through the house and flung open the parlor door. But the room had been cold, empty, and quiet.

The storm raged on through the night. A spiteful wind threw sand against Hattie Belle's bedroom window, threatening, screaming with coarse laughter. After a long time she fell into a fitful sleep. Her eyes had hardly closed, it seemed, when over the roar of the wind she heard two sharp raps on her bedroom door. "Yes?" she said sleepily.

"It's past seven o'clock," her stepmother said, raising her voice to be heard above the noise of the storm. "How late do you intend to stay abed? I could use some help with breakfast."

"I'll get right up," Hattie Belle answered in a voice blurred with sleep, but when she opened her eyes, she saw no morning light coming through the windows. As a heavy wind beat against the glass, a chill of fear ran through her. She had never seen a day when the sun didn't rise.

She reached for her clothes on a chair near the bed, dressed quickly under the covers, and got her hair in place with the aid of brush and tortoise shell pins. She opened the bedroom door, then turned and picked up her reticule filled with Lemmie's letters. Maybe they would help her hope again.

Mary had emptied the contents of the beanpot into the big iron spider. Usually the rich aroma of the baked beans bubbling on top of the stove, was a welcome one. Today it made her feel sick to her stomach.

After washing her hands and splashing cold water on her face, Hattie Belle sliced thick rounds of brown bread, spread them with butter, then placed them on a flat pan to toast in the oven.

"I've been waiting for a break in the storm," Captain Davis said. "Got to get out to feed the animals soon. They'll be angry now, moving about and stamping their feet. Hope they don't break something."

Once seated at the table, Captain Davis nodded toward Hattie Belle for her to say grace. She said the one that her mother used to say in the days when she, not Mary, had sat directly across the table.

"Lord Jesus be our Holy Guest
Our morning joy, our evening rest.
And with this daily bread impart
Thy love and peace to every heart."

The wind screamed like a maniac, bent on the destruction of every living thing. The meal passed in silence.

"I wish we could move away from here," Mary finally said, as she finished her second cup of tea.

The muscles at the corners of Captain Davis' mouth tightened. After awhile he said, "This old salt is used to waking to the call of seabirds. I count on watching the rising sun lay a path across the water. I count on smelling the good, clean salt air. At day's end, I like to amble down to the shore, study the stars, and listen to the water as it laps against the rocks."

"You're talking about times when the water behaves," Mary said. "What about times like today, when the sea brings a dreadful hurricane with it?"

Does she really want to move from here because of the storms that blow in off the sea? Hattie Belle asked herself. Or is it because she hates this house, which she knows holds a thousand memories of another wife?

Captain Davis frowned and tapped his fingers on the table. "Mary, I say there is no better place in the world to live than right here." He turned to Hattie Belle, and above the roar of the wind said, "I'm giving you an acre of land on the main road as a wedding present. Lem can build you a home there."

"Oh thank you, Papa," she said, a vibrancy in her voice. "I know Lemmie will be as pleased as I am." She knew almost exactly where it would be, as the land was owned in strips across the peninsula. She wanted to walk around the table and give him a hug, but she knew Mary wouldn't like it.

After a few minutes some of her happiness faded as she silently reminded herself that she mustn't count on his return.

The shrieking and howling of the wind lessened a bit, as if nature no longer had the energy to continue its outrageous attacks. "The storm must be coming to an end, Papa," Hattie Belle said, as she and Captain Davis stood at the kitchen window. "The wind isn't nearly as wild as it was. Look—the sky is changing from black to grey."

As the sky grew even lighter, Mary came over to peer out the window. "It's a strange sight out there. Over near the piazza and along the stone wall I see drifts higher than a man's head. But I also see spots of bare ground swept clean by the wind."

"And everything is quiet except for the water," Hattie Belle added. "It's still wild."

"Time I took care of the animals," Captain Davis said. "Not sure the storm has ended for good, though." As he headed for the back hall where his heavy clothes and boots were kept, he added, "Find me those old clotheslines, Mary."

When she brought them, he fastened them together with seaman's knots, tied one end of the rope around his waist, and when he went outside attached the other to the clothesline hook by the door. He picked up the milk pails and headed for the barn.

"Well, good weather or bad, there are dishes to do," Mary said.

My job of course, Hattie Belle said to herself. She was almost finished with the pans when she saw the sky change color. "Mother!" she called. "Look!"

"Oh my!" Mary said. As they watched, the sky began to darken again, and the wind to bend the trees. "Run, Hattie Belle! Open the side door. I'll bring a lantern."

Once Hattie Belle had unlatched the door, it banged open and almost knocked her down. The Captain, staggered in, his head bleeding, and fell to the floor.

Hattie Belle reached outside and took the line off the hook, then she and Mary pushed with all their might to shut the door. The Captain still lay on the floor, trying to get his breath. "Didn't know as I'd make it," he gasped. They helped him to his feet, then got him settled in his rocking chair.

Hattie Belle covered him with a quilt, and Mary washed the blood from his face. "Wind knocked me over," he said. "I fell against the well. Bumped my head. Spilled both buckets of milk. Hard to get on my feet again."

He gave a tremendous sneeze. "Chilled clear through," he groaned. "Coming down with a heavy cold. Only sure cure is a rum sweat. Get me a kettle of steaming water. Make a tent."

Hattie Belle pulled two chairs away from their places at the table, put them back to back, about three feet apart, and spread a quilt over them. When the water began to boil, Mary pushed a small braided rug beneath the chairs, and put the steaming kettle of water on it. The captain carefully placed his bottle of rum inside the tent and crawled in after it.

Hattie Belle wondered what it must be like at sea if the wind was so strong that even on land it could blow her father off his feet. Depressed, she picked up her mother's Bible and leafed through it, looking for inspiration. She turned to Psalm 107, and began with the 23rd verse.

"They that go down to the sea in ships, that do business in great waters.

These see the works of the Lord, and his wonders in the deep.

For he commandeth, and raiseth the stormy wind, which lifteth up the waves thereof.

They mount up to heaven, they go down again to the depths: their soul is melted because of trouble.

They reel to and fro, and stagger like a drunken man, and are at their wit's end.

Then they cry unto the Lord in their trouble, and he bringeth them out of their distresses."

Outside, the wind shrieked about the house. Waves crashed against the shore.

Oh Lord, please hear the cries of those aboard the *Scorpion*! Hattie Belle prayed. Scenes from her nightmare were always at the edge of her mind.

His letters, although a poor substitute for being in his arms, were of great importance to her—their only means of communication. She'd saved all of them since their engagement in the spring of '96. Those written aboard the Snow schooner *E. Arcularius*, were from Perth Amboy, New Jersey; Wiscasset, Maine; New York City. Although he would mention the loads of lime, coal or lumber, and how much they brought, the parts she had re-read most often were those that said, "I miss you" and "I love you."

The most exciting letters would be when he wrote to tell her when he'd be home and would come calling. But she remembered the day he appeared unannounced at her boarding house—in January of '97. She was still at Pemaquid Point, living with a different family than when he had last visited. Although he hadn't written, she had expected him.

Hattie Belle had read with heavy heart the newspaper account of his sister May's death—a child she had grown very fond of when she boarded at the Brown's home in Walpole. The brilliant girl had also been one of her pupils in the village's one room schoolhouse.

After reading the newspaper, Hattie Belle had sat at her writing table for a long time. She tried over and over to write a note of sympathy to the Browns, fully aware of how inadequate any attempts at consolation must be. Nothing she wrote seemed right. She finally asked the landlady which letter she most approved of, bowed to her judgement, and sent it.

Hattie Belle could still see Lemmie as he stood in the doorway of the boarding house, his dark eyes filled with grief, his sweeping mustache icy from the vapor fog that had frozen on it. A heavy haze blurred her view of his sleigh, blanket covered horses, and the woods across the road. He asked if she might like to go for a walk.

Snow crunched beneath their feet, and she heard from a distance the ringing of the fog bell and the roar of the surf as it crashed against the rocks below the lighthouse.

They hadn't walked far from the boarding house, when it disappeared behind curtains of Arctic fog, and they were alone in a veil of mist. He held her close. "May was only 16, Hattie," he said thickly. "Only 16."

The fog had created such a feeling of unreality, that for just a second it seemed but a dream, from which she would awaken, and know that his little sister was going about her studies in Boston.

As reality crowded back, and Hattie Belle hunted for comforting words, the pain she had felt three years ago, after the loss of her own sister May to consumption, came rushing back. After a few minutes she managed to say, "She has gone on to a better life, Lemmie. We know she is happy because she is with the Lord."

"Yes," he said with a deep sigh, "but she leaves such an empty place here."

During the rest of '97 and into the spring of '98 she saw him on the average of once every two months. On his last visit, in early April, they had made plans to get married on the second Sunday in June. Two weeks later, however, a letter that could never have been foreseen, arrived. The envelope had a New York postmark, and seemingly in haste, he had scrawled to the left of it, "New York Navy Yard, Brooklyn." The date at the top of the first page was April 15, 1898. She would never forget what it said.

Chapter 11

War

Hattie Belle

"Hattie, my Love,

"I want you to burn this letter as soon as you finish it, and never tell another living soul the contents. You will hardly believe what I have to tell you. I can't believe it myself. Strange circumstances have forced me to join the navy to save my skin. It all began after my deckhand came down with pneumonia and had to be sent home. I went to the agency to hire another man. The fellow I was given wore a continual greasy smile, and I didn't like the looks of him. But because we were leaving on the next tide and were a man short, I put my doubts aside and hired him.

"He turned out to be a lazy good-for-nothing that didn't half do his work. We had sailed into New York Harbor, and the other men had gone ashore. I wanted to leave the vessel myself, to sign the papers to get my cargo unloaded, and then to meet Lawrence, who I knew was also in port.

"But I kept this fellow back and began giving him a good dressing down. All of a sudden he turned, picked up a marlin spike, and threw it at me. As it whizzed past my head, I knew he meant to kill me. Acting out of fear, I grabbed up that spike and hurled it back at him. It hit him in the groin and he collapsed, screaming in pain. Terrified at what I had done, I ran to a shipping agency to find a telephone. When I told the clerk there had been an accident aboard my ship, he called an ambulance for me.

"I raced back to my schooner and found my brother Lawrence standing on the wharf in front of her, a worried look on his face. Never was I so glad to see him. In some way I can't explain, we always know when the other is in trouble. When I told him what had happened, he climbed up the gangway, pulled the marlin spike from the now unconscious seaman, and threw it overboard.

"When the ambulance had left, and the clatter from the wagon wheels and horses' hooves had faded, I said, 'Lawrence, I've got to find a telephone where I won't be overheard, and call the Company.' When I told Mr. Snow what had happened, he was sympathetic and said he'd send his lawyer from Rockland should I need him.

"After I'd hung up the phone, Lawrence said we should now get together with several captain friends, whose vessels were along the waterfront. They might have an idea as to what I should do.

"All of them felt there was plenty of reason to worry. Of late there has been a public outcry on behalf of sailors who found themselves at the mercy of brutal captains on what sailors call 'Hell Ships.' Because there had been no witnesses to what happened aboard my schooner, my friends believed that there would be a trial. If he died, I might go to jail.

"One of the captains said he thought I should immediately get myself over to Brooklyn and sign up with the Navy. The others agreed it was the only safe way out. I called the Snow Company again, and Mr. Snow told me to go ahead. He would send another captain for the schooner.

"Lawrence went with me to the Navy Yard for support. I could hardly believe the strange twist my life had taken. He cautioned me not to tell that I was a captain, but to just say I'd had some experience at sea. He reasoned that the enlistment officer would be curious as to why a person in command of a coastal vessel would be anxious to join the navy as a lowly seaman. And if the deckhand died, and the authorities came asking questions, the enlistment officer would remember a captain.

"As it was, I'm sure I looked like a fellow down on his luck. I hadn't had time to go to the barber's, so I was in bad need of a haircut and shave.

"To sign up, I went aboard the U.S. Receiving-Ship Vermont, a 74-gun three-master which lies here in the Navy Yard. The enlisting officer asked me to explain 'Boxing the Compass,' and several other elemental questions on seamanship. He seemed pleased with my answers and said, 'You'll get your training right here on this vessel.'

"This is the worst part, Hattie—I had to sign up for a year. I plan, though, to find some way to get a military discharge after a few months. How could all this have happened to me in just a couple of hours? I feel as if I'm in the middle of a nightmare.

"You don't know how much I hate putting off our marriage. If I can find any good in this situation, it's that I'll be able to save toward building a house of our own. The pay is good—$19 a month—and I'll put back every cent. Say a few prayers that the fellow who tried to kill me doesn't die. The thought of going to jail is terrible."

Shaking and sick to her stomach, she had read it over and over, unwilling to believe what had happened. Finally she threw the letter into the woodstove and watched it burn.

Each day as she read the papers, she felt more and more convinced that war was on the way. During the Cuban civil war, our country's sympathies had been with the native people instead of the ruling Spaniards. In the middle of February, when our ship, the *Maine*, had been sunk in Havana Harbor, with great loss of American life, tempers flared.

Missionaries sent back reports telling how the Spanish soldiers, acting under orders, had set fire to the thatched houses of the country people, and when they ran out to keep from being roasted alive, they were herded into towns which didn't have enough food to feed them. As a result, many were starving.

Editorials urging war against Spain compared the murder of the Cubans by the Spanish to the murder of the Armenians by the Turks.

The day following the U.S. declaration of war against Spain, the front page stories shouted that "McKinley Proclaims Blockade of Cuba." Then in somewhat smaller letters, "All ships attempting to enter Havana, or other northern ports, are liable to seizure."

"Oh dear!" she said, as she put down the paper. "Now what will happen to Lemmie?"

A letter dated Saturday, April 30, held the answer. It upset her almost as much as the one in which he told her about having to join the Navy.

"Hattie, my Love,

"I'm on the Scorpion now, a yacht made over into a warship. At 1:30 p.m. we started taking on ammunition, finishing at 4:30. At 4:40 we cast off moorings, stood out of the Navy Yard, then down the river and through the channel for the open sea. At 6 p.m. Sandy Hook Light House bore abeam. We're making passage for Fortress Monroe in Virginia.

"Now that the blockade has been declared, there is no way I can get a discharge, so we may as well accept the situation. Keep sending your letters addressed to the Scorpion, care of the New York Navy Yard, and I'll get them eventually.

"All my love always,

Lem"

The storm outside, like the storm in her heart, was getting worse. Would either of them never end? She heard a tremendous crash against the far side of the house. Captain Davis threw open the dining room door and started running toward the front hall, then up the front stairs. Mary followed. Hattie Belle believed it must be a major part of the old pear tree.

She used the time they were gone to take Lemmie's letters out of her reticule and file them between the pages of Mama's Bible.

She began reading a letter written early in May.

"Hattie, my Love,

"Sure do like that picture of you in your new Sunday bonnet. When we're married, I don't know if I'll be able to concentrate on Godly things when I see you up there in the front of the church playing the organ or singing a solo. I've looked at your picture so often, I think I may wear it out.

"We are off Hampton Roads, Virginia, as I write. I think we may stay here during the war because it's a good place to protect the coast from Spanish attack. Last night it was our duty to stop everything in and out of the capes all night long. How the men on the bay boats swore as our vessel pulled alongside. Strange, but we didn't come across a single Spaniard."

The next letter, written in the middle of May, was hidden in Proverbs.

"Hattie, my Love,

"I spent the last two days in the brig, where I dined on bread and water. I'm afraid my quick temper got the better of me. The most bullying of the officers swore at me for something I didn't do. I kept calm, but when he said nasty things about my mother, I took a swing at him.

"We're between Thimble Shoals light and Cape Henry light today. We've joined the Flying Squadron and are getting ready for duty in the Caribbean. This morning we had sub-calibre target practice with 6 pounder guns."

Hattie Belle heard the footsteps of Captain Davis and Mary as they started back down the stairs, and quickly turned to a part of the Bible that had no letters from Lemmie.

"Not much damage to the inside wall," Captain Davis said, "but I'll bet the outside one will need considerable repair. I hope it won't be as costly as the repairs we had to made last June when lightning struck."

Hattie Belle felt a sudden sadness, remembering how that was supposed to have been her special day—the day she and Lemmie had planned to be married. No one had mentioned how sorry they were. Had they felt that to call attention to it would only make her feel worse, or had they completely forgotten? That morning they had spoken only of the expected summer people, and such things as how the long time guests from Darien, Connecticut would enjoy the improved looks of their freshly painted bedroom and the new curtains. She'd felt like screaming.

The tempest had begun in the afternoon. The thunder was loud, and a steady stream of light stayed around the house. All of a sudden it grew black. "Quick!" Captain Davis had shouted, "Chairs against the wall! Feet on the rungs!" Within seconds, fire came down the chimney. It took the form of a huge orange ball about two feet high, and bounced up and down as if it were of rubber. Then, with a bang, it exploded, leaving everyone both blind and deaf for several minutes. When at last their senses returned, they saw the air was filled with blue smoke. The stove lids were turned on their sides, and all the tacks in the zinc pad beneath the stove had been pulled out. A black line was burned around the top of the walls, just below the ceiling. They ran from room to room, expecting fire. In the front room, all the gold was gone from the wallpaper, leaving the appearance of white sheets. The small stove had its pipe pulled from the wall.

They raced to the second floor. Every room was filled with blue smoke which had the smell of sulfur. They ran up the steps to the attic. Great gashes were sliced in the beams, but no fire, thank goodness.

Downstairs, over the iron sink, they found a small hole, about as big around as a pencil, from which the lightning had escaped.

The adventure had left Hattie Belle feeling weary, but somehow emotionally satisfied. She had not been able to act out her frustration, but nature had done it for her with a monumental tantrum.

Outside, the wind still roared, as the storm continued. Would Lemmie come home, and would they have the love she longed for?

For Sunday night supper they had what Captain Davis called "Cape Cod Turkcy": creamed salt codfish over potatoes—a tasty dish. Captain Davis, his eyebrows knit in a frown, ate slowly, a faraway look in his eyes. "I can feel what it's like out there," he said. "On the way to China another fellow and I were on a masthead, fifty feet above the deck, when a wave shot over us. Somehow I held on, but my friend fell to his death. I imagine a number of such tragedies are happening right now. I expect that when the mail comes, I'll see in the paper the name of a captain or two, that I know, listed among those lost."

(Courtesy of the Mariners Museum at Newport News)
U.S.S. SCORPION

The kitchen had gradually filled with the delightful smell of his favorite dessert, apple pie, and as he became aware of it, and turned to look in the direction of the stove, some of the tension left his face. Mary took the pie out of the oven, and cut him a generous serving. He ate it with obvious pleasure, savoring each bite. "It's wicked good, Mary," he said when he finished, and handed back his plate for another piece.

As Hattie Belle cleared the table, she pretended that she and Lemmie were married and in their own home on Pemaquid Harbor Road. But after awhile her fears returned. Would he really come back?

"The wind is lighter right now," Captain Davis, said over his shoulder as he went to the back hallway for in his heavy clothes. "I can't put off the milking any longer." He once again tied the rope around his waist, and started out with a lit lantern in one hand and the milk pail handles in the other.

When he returned from the barn, carrying the milk pails, he sank into his chair, exhausted. "Hard to get those barn doors open," he said. "If the storm has petered out in the morning, I think I'll put on my snowshoes and try to get up to the post office. Even though the mail carrier won't be able to get through, people will be there, maybe buying kerosene or matches, but mostly just talking.

Maybe someone will have heard something about the *Chamberlain*. "I hope all the Brown boys will make it through!"

All the Brown boys! Hattie Belle thought. I've been concentrating so much on Lemmie, that I've hardly thought of Percy and Lawrence, or even poor Myrtie Belle. I know her parents are suffering too.

She thought about how frightened and seasick Myrtie Belle must be. She had heard that the young bride was not happy on the water even in good weather.

"Still bad outside," he said. "I wonder if the *Chamberlain* will make it. I wonder about the *Robert A. Snow* and the *Addie E. Snow*."

"And the *Scorpion*," Hattie Belle said.

About an hour later Captain Davis and Mary started up the back stairway with a lantern and their hot flatirons, but Hattie Belle didn't think she could sleep. Her stomach gnawed with anxiety. After a while there came a lull in the storm, and Hattie Belle stood at the window looking out into the moonlight. A large moose stood motionless on the bank, evidently resting after a long haul through the deep snow and crust—a beautiful and lonely sight against the full moon and the dark water of the harbor.

Chapter 12

North Station

Delia

The great winds that followed the sea grew fiercer, screaming unintelligible curses as they beat against the walls of North Station. They forced their icy breath through the invisible cracks between walls and windows.

"You're shivering, Deal," Frank said as he wrapped her fur cape around her shoulders. Several women, who sat near windows, covered themselves with their long wool cloaks.

There was a continual cold draft as poor people came in to get out of the weather, along with those whose homes had been made unliveable by the storm.

Mary and Joshua Adams, pleasant acquaintances of only a few hours, sat just across the aisle from Frank. Their three-month-old baby was crying again. Her wails, coming in high pitched waves, gave a background of raw intensity to Delia's memory of her dreadful vision. She re-lived it again and again: the misty outline of a great steamer, rolling and pitching; the screams of passengers as huge waves destroyed the superstructure; and the clear view of the small schooner, with the sailor tied to the wheel, as the two vessels crashed into each other.

Who was that young man? Delia asked herself over and over until she thought she must lose her mind. The vision of the schooner and steamship had not allowed her to see the face of the sailor. Was he one of Frank's nephews who made his living as a coastal sea captain, or one of her own seafaring nephews?

Frank's face was grim, and she knew had the same questions.

"If only I'd seen his face, Frank."

He took her hand and held it tight. "Maybe it's better that we don't know."

A tense male voice, to Delia's right, asked, "Will that baby never stop?"

Delia had been only vaguely aware that someone had moved into the space beside her. When she turned her head toward the voice, she saw a young man of perhaps 19, his eyes glazed with pain. A jagged red scar ran down one side of his face, and one pant leg hung empty. Crutches leaned against his chair.

"I hope she'll stop soon," Delia answered in a low voice. The brief exchange with the suffering young man had brought her back to the present, and she became fully aware of those who sat close by. On the other side of the suffering young man was a grey-haired woman who was knitting something red, a mitten, maybe. She appeared to be in half-mourning, dressed entirely in black except for a white crocheted collar at her neck. Beside her were two little girls, perhaps three and four. Each held a small, rudely carved wooden doll.

Delia glanced across at the Adams family. Beyond them were two elderly men in plaid shirts and work pants, talking with each other. She overheard the stout one saying something about his son at sea.

A strange looking fellow came by and asked if he could sit next to Frank, so Delia and the young man moved down a bit, and the grey haired woman with two small children moved directly across the aisle. In addition to constantly smiling to himself, he wore an odd mix of clothing. His faded and much patched shirt and pants seemed more suitable for working in a barn than for wearing on a train trip. But he also wore a new-looking black suit coat with a velvet collar, similar in style to Frank's.

From outside came a monstrous roar, as though from some great, primitive beast. The toddler began to cry.

The oddly dressed fellow, however, seemed not to have heard the great roar of the storm or the crying child. He continued to stare straight ahead with the same unwavering smile.

"I went to the Mechanics Fair," he finally blurted out, to no one in particular. "Sure was nice. Heard lots of good music and speeches. I liked the exhibits, too. Don't know but what I liked the billiard and pool exhibit best. They had electric cushion tables. Never saw anything like it." Suddenly he looked embarrassed, as though he shouldn't have spoken. "I don't get away from home much," he said. "I reckon you all have been there."

"No, I haven't," Frank said. "I live in East Boston, but I've never had the chance to go."

The fellow began smiling again, and shifted in the seat to look directly at Frank. "I was just lucky. My sister sent me the money for the tickets.

Cora has a good job doing piece work in a garment factory, and she saved up. I didn't want to take the money at first, but she said that us getting together was a present for her, too."

"Why, that was a mighty fine thing for her to do," Frank said.

Oh dear! Delia thought. A good job? When May had lived with them, and had seemed to grow more and more tired, Frank had taken a day off his work as a stevedore and gone with Delia to the factory where the girl worked. They demanded that she come home. Delia hadn't forgotten the dreariness, the crowded conditions, and the hopeless looks on the faces of the women, who worked long hours for small pay. She could imagine the sacrifices this man's sister had made, cutting back on food and fuel.

"I didn't want her to have to buy my eats," he continued, "so I brought along a big piece of salt codfish and a bag of potatoes that a farmer give me for helping him dig a ditch. He loaned me his good suit coat, too. Said he wanted me to look my best when I got to Boston and saw my sister."

"Nice looking coat," Frank said. "You could wear it to the best places."

"Well, I did. Last night we went all over Boston—visited the big churches, looked into the fancy restaurants and fine shops. Cora and I had a grand time together." Then his forehead knotted into a frown. "I'm kind of worried now, though, about staying here overnight. I left a dime with a boy down the road so he could feed my dog when I was gone. I wasn't figuring on staying the extra time."

"When he sees how bad the storm is, he'll know you can't travel in it," Frank said. "He'll keep taking care of your dog till you get back. Then you can pay him a bit more."

"Ayuh, I reckon that's how it will be," he said, as a look of relief flooded over his face. "That dog is mighty special to me. Back home in Maine, he's all the family I've got."

"You never married," Delia said.

"Yes, I did. I got married in the spring of '61. Sally had just turned 17 and I'd turned 18 a couple months before. I had a parcel of land my uncle left me, and I farmed it. A run-down cabin sat on the property, but she fixed it up pretty.

"I didn't want to go to war, didn't want to leave my wife and my home. But the town folks started calling me a slacker, so I enlisted in August of '62. They said it would all be over in a few months.

"But I didn't get to go home until two years later, and on account of being bad wounded. It happened when I was in the Battle of the Wilderness. The flashes from the guns set the woods afire right near me. I run then, carrying my friend Ben. Didn't think of anything but getting away from the fire—forgot to be careful. That was when one of Lee's boys shot me in the head." He took a deep breath. "That's what I tell people. But maybe it wasn't one of them that did it. Our units got all mixed up in the woods, and by accident some of us shot at our own men." He pointed to an indented spot above his right ear. "Bullet's still in there. 'I don't dare take it out,' the surgeon said...'too close to the brain.'"

The young man, with the scar and missing leg, leaned forward a bit. "Have much pain?"

"No. It feels like something is pressing hard inside my head...always pressing. But I do pretty well if I don't get upset." For a short time he stopped talking and looked off toward the window, where the storm still shouted and threatened.

"I wasn't back home two weeks when I lost my wife," he said.

The grey haired woman, looked up from her knitting and sighed audibly. "Did you lose your wife to consumption?" she asked. "That's how I lost my daughter. It was six months ago today."

"No. That wasn't what happened. She run off. Told people she was afraid of me...said I hit her. I don't remember doing it, but if she said I did...." He paused and looked across at the toddler in the sailor dress and red stockings, perched on Joshua Adams' knee. "She'd taken the baby with her."

The two elderly men looked at each other and shook their heads. The heavy set one moved his chaw of tobacco to the other side of his mouth. "Mighty hard luck," he said.

"I'll say," the thin one muttered.

A murmur of agreement traveled along the two benches.

After a few minutes, the man who'd fought in the Battle of the Wilderness sat up straighter, and lifted his chin. "I keep in touch with my boy. I lost my land because I couldn't pay the taxes, but I do odd jobs and save up, and there's never been a Christmas I haven't been able to send him a dollar. I'm not real good at writing, so the farmer up the road does the envelope for me. Then on the paper I've wrapped the dollar in, he puts, 'From your father,' and I sign my name."

"That's a fine thing, keeping in touch with your boy," Frank said.

Delia held back tears. The War of the Rebellion had been over thirty years ago. She wondered if his son ever wrote to say thank you or to inquire about his father's health, but she didn't dare ask.

The toddler began fussing, but stopped for a bit when Frank put a shiny penny in his hand. The baby's crying continued.

Delia, nerves at the breaking point, jumped up without planning to, and heard herself saying, "Let me hold her for you, Mrs. Adams. I'll walk with her and see if that helps. You try to get some sleep."

In the jiggling of the infant, as the mother handed her to Delia, the baby gave a loud burp, followed by several others. She then relaxed, closed her eyes, and almost immediately fell asleep.

The feel of the warm little body, the sight of the innocent face, with its moist, dewy skin; and the smell of roses around the infant's hairline took her back to a long ago time when she was a young woman living in St. John. One fall, her older sister, Faith, whose husband was at sea, had come home with her new baby, the first of that generation. The sister, who had almost died when the child was born, looked terribly thin and drawn, but the baby was plump and rosy. Giving life could have a high price.

During the coming weeks, Delia's mother had taken care of the older daughter, making her nourishing soups and puddings; and all the while keeping her warm inside with hot tea, and outside with thick comforters. Delia had taken charge of the baby.

In the years that followed, she'd always had a special feeling for that boy. She reflected that the infant she held in her arms that cold November day was now grown and a mariner. Then a terrible thought stabbed its way into her heart. Could he be the young man she had seen in the vision—tied to a small schooner's steering wheel—and headed for certain death? A sob rose in her throat, but she took a deep breath and swallowed it.

The ticket agent, who'd been pacing about the room, stopped to talk. "We're lucky to be on land tonight. It's bad on the water. Just before the telephone lines went down, a railroad friend called from Cape Cod. He said the sea there was a wild sight, covered with foam for several miles off shore."

"I don't doubt it," Joshua said. "I'd hate to be off there tonight."

"It's not called the Sailor's Graveyard for nothing," Frank added.

"Oh God," the stout man in the plaid shirt said. "I hope my boy's not near there."

The pale young man, who'd lost a leg, leaned forward, grimacing in pain as he did. "I came pretty close to checking out a while back, but it wasn't on the water."

"In the Spanish War?" Frank asked.

"Right."

"A brave young man," Frank said.

"Maybe I was once, but I'm acting the coward tonight. I'm running away from my duty. I'm supposed to stay here in Boston. I'm supposed to testify before the War Investigating Board.

"It's going to be at the Parker House on Monday. A lot of people are angry at how bad our wounded men were treated. They think that with decent care, a lot more soldiers could have lived. I've heard that those looked after by Clara Barton and her nurses did well. Most of us weren't that lucky."

Frowning, he rubbed his hands agitatedly back and forth along the wooden seat. "I don't feel up to testifying. They'd most likely ask me hundreds of questions. They'd be trying to decide if I was telling the truth, maybe trying to trick me. There was a time when it wouldn't have bothered me. But my nerves are too shot now. I feel as if I might break down."

"I reckon you've been through some mighty bad times," Frank said.

The soldier with the missing leg nodded. "Yup. Funny thing. When I first saw the coast of Cuba, I thought it was the prettiest place I'd ever seen. I saw a dark line of palm trees, a border of silvery sand, and a kind of soft blue-green sea. That's all the good I can remember about Cuba...that first look from far away."

"The fighting must have been bad," Frank said.

"You're right about that, Mister. A lot of us got wounded. A friend carried me on his shoulders to a field hospital near El Caney. Others were taken in blankets. It was just to a piece of ground under a big tree, and directly behind the firing line.

"The ground was damp from the rain, it seemed to rain all the time, and we were being eaten alive by mosquitoes. We sure were glad when wagons came in the night to take us to the hospital in Siboney. We didn't know how much we would suffer on the way."

Every eye was on the young veteran, and although the storm outside snarled in hatred, and screamed its endless threats, people gave their attention to the soldier and his account of those wounded in the war.

"They loaded us into springless wagons without even any straw in the bottom," he continued. "I can still feel how rough and splintered the floor and sides were."

"Rough and splintered?" Joshua said.

"Yes, because of the weight of those heavy barrels, cartridge boxes and other freight they'd carried that day. And there weren't any compartments, the way there are in ambulances, so there wasn't a thing for us to hold onto. We were rolled and tossed about as the wagons jolted over what seemed to be bushes and rocks."

"Driving blind in the dark," Frank commented.

"Right. There were also several streams that had to be crossed, and when the wagons plunged down the banks of one, the air was filled with moans. There would be a wait then, because the wheels got stuck in the heavy mud, then suddenly the wagons would be pulled in a hurry up the other side.

"One of the fellows, who'd been shot in the stomach, cried out several times, 'Stop! Stop! For God's sake!' But the drivers kept going. By the time we got to the hospital at Siboney we were all in a heap. No one was strong enough to get himself free.

"When they lifted us out, we were covered with splinters...some deep inside our skin. Several of the men were dead."

From outside North Station came a blast so loud it seemed like the roar from a hundred great guns. People cried out, and covered their ears.

The man who'd fought in the Battle of the Wilderness jumped to his feet. "The woods are afire!" he screamed. "We've got to get out of here! Come on, Ben—you'll be burned alive!"

Frank stood up and put a hand on his shoulder. "That was a long time ago," he said kindly. "You're in Boston now. You've been having a grand time visiting your sister, remember?" But when the fellow looked around the station, then back at Frank, his eyes were filled with confusion. He finally sat down, and stared off into the past.

A sweat had broken out on the forehead of the young man who'd fought in the war with Spain, and his hands trembled as he tried to light his pipe. Frank lit it for him.

The soldier closed his eyes and smoked for a few minutes before going on with his story about the Spanish War. "I remember that first night, how we kept calling for water, but the men in the next tent, who were supposed to be our nurses, just shouted, 'Shut up.'"

"Heartless wretches!" said the heavy set man whose son was at sea. "Should have been horsewhipped." The others nodded in agreement.

The young man puffed on his pipe for a bit. "You think I'm doing a bad thing, leaving, not going to testify? I don't want to be called a quitter, but I don't think I can do it." He began trembling again.

"You're doing just right," Frank said. "There will be others, not as bad wounded, who can testify."

"Where are you headed?" Joshua asked.

"Deer Isle, Maine. Got a brother there. He'll see me through till I get my strength back. I'll probably be baitman on his lobster boat—after awhile."

Deer Isle, Delia repeated to herself. That's in East Penobscot Bay, where the granite isles are. In the letter from Percy that came yesterday, he said that he had become captain of the schooner *Addie E. Snow*, and would be leaving in a few days from one of those islands, I forget the name, bound for New York and carrying stone. Was the mention of Deer Isle an omen ... a sign that he was the one I saw in the schooner with the broken masts? Oh ... I don't know ... I can't think straight.

The young veteran, who'd lost a leg, closed his eyes and grimaced with pain. "I need my laudanum now. It's in my coat pocket," he said, trying to feel around behind his back, "but I can't find my coat."

Frank found it where it had slipped off onto the floor. In addition to the bottle of medicine in one of the pockets, he found some small change. He added a dollar bill.

"I don't want charity," the wounded man said, watching.

"This isn't charity," Frank told him. "This is in gratitude for what you've suffered for your country."

"Oh," he said, and there was a suggestion of a smile at one corner of his mouth. A short while after he took his medicine, his face relaxed and his eyes closed.

"Poor lad," the grey haired woman said, "but he did his duty, and he can be proud of that. When my daughter died, her husband, the father of these girls, said he was leaving, and I could raise his children. He left in the night without so much as a fare thee well to the girls. A cousin of mine, who lives in New Bedford, wrote that he'd been seen there, signing on to a whaler."

Joshua's wife, Mary, hugged her baby closer, a disturbed look in her eyes. "He left a note, I expect?"

"No."

"Some money, I hope?" Joshua said.

"Not a cent. And I've run out of what little I'd saved."

"The rascal ought to be horsewhipped!" the heavy set man again offered as a fit punishment.

"Too good for him," his friend said.

"My sister and her husband live on a farm," the grandmother said, "and she wrote that they'll take us in. Ida's not well, and needs someone to take care of her and do the cooking and cleaning." She put the nearly finished mitten in her reticule and began covering the girls with their coats. "Close your eyes now," she said to them.

As Delia pulled her cape higher around her shoulders, in preparation for her own sleep, she looked at the people once again, and thought of the troubled lives most of them had...lives with no happy ending in sight.

Sleep was impossible. Whenever Delia began drifting off, the thin fellow in the plaid shirt gave a tremendous snort followed by the high pitched laughter of the little girls. The grandmother didn't criticize them or tell them to be quiet. Perhaps it sounded good to her. There had been little enough to laugh about in the past few months.

The stout fellow in the plaid shirt made no attempt at sleep, but sat chewing his tobacco, deep lines of worry on his face as he thought of his son at sea. From time to time he spat into a nearby spittoon.

At six a.m. complete silence reigned outside, and faint rays of light came through the windows.

"Now the trains can run," someone cried. Others cheered.

"I wouldn't be surprised if it's the eye of the storm passing over," Joshua said.

"Aye," Frank agreed.

Within a short while, the storm started again. Around 9 o'clock the wind suddenly became its wildest yet, screaming in uncontrollable rage.

"My son, Josiah, is captain of a coal barge," the stout fellow in the plaid shirt said. "I hope to God he'll make it through."

"We'll pray for him," the grandmother said. She bowed her head, and her lips moved in prayer. Others followed her lead.

"I hope God helps him," Frank murmured to Delia, "and our nephews who are out there, too."

Delia thought of the desperate fellow at the wheel, and said a prayer for his soul.

The ticket agent passed around a tray of stale doughnuts.

"Not much like our good breakfasts at home, with fried fish, hot biscuits and baked apples," Frank said to Delia. "But right now we're lucky to have anything." He looked thoughtful. "I've been wondering how our neighbor's fishing boat is standing up to the storm. Don't know what Richard would do if anything happened to her."

"He and May Belle might lose their home," Delia said.

Sometime after ten, the raving and shrieking outside let up a little, but the snow kept beating against the windows.

Chapter 13

Tony Angelo

A couple of trains arrived in the late morning with reports of flooding, washouts, plus downed poles and wires. All outgoing trains were cancelled.

In the early afternoon a group of people, composed of two theatrical companies, entered the waiting room, planning to take trains to far away cities. When told they couldn't get a train, they at first thought it was a joke, but then got upset when they learned they might not get to their Monday performances.

The tension was broken when a drunken fellow staggered in and began singing. His voice was not professional, but people began to chuckle and sang along with him.

In the middle of the afternoon a young man in heavy clothes and a dark stocking cap strode in.

"Hey," he said. "I'm Tony Angelo. I got a double sleigh and a team of horses. Anybody wants to go back home, I take. I don't charge much." He pulled off his cap and ran his fingers through his curly black hair.

"How is it out there?" Frank called out.

"Wind not so heavy now—wearing down. But sea runs high. Schooners and coal barges—they pile up against pier heads. Others stuck on islands and rocks. Some sink."

"Coal barges?" the stout man in the plaid shirt said. "My son...."

Joshua leaned forward. "If he's a canny mariner, he'll have known the gale was coming. I'll bet he and his crew are in a tavern somewhere in Boston, eating some good beef and spinning yarns."

The stout man almost smiled. "I think you're right. Yes sir, that's just about what he would do."

"Anybody want a ride?" the young fellow asked.

Frank jumped to his feet, signaling with a wave of his hand that they would go. Then, looking down at his wife, said, "I'll be needed, Deal. Maybe I can help save some cargo on those wrecked vessels. We'll go home first; then when the water grows calmer, I'll see what I can do."

"Do you think it's safe to leave?" Delia asked.

"Safe now," Tony said. "Snow still falls, but wind not so hard."

Delia tied her scarf around her head, and fastened the neck of her fur cape. "I hate to think of what the storm may have done to our house."

"We need to go to 29 Falcon Street in East Boston," Frank said to the young man. "Do you think you can get us way up there near Chelsea Creek? I'll pay you well, if you do."

"First we get to Atlantic Avenue, and if the North Ferry runs, I get you home all right. Maybe I am gone so long that my Rose worries and says her beads. But we need extra money. Baby comes soon."

While Tony picked up their three valises and took them outside, Delia and Frank made their way along the waiting room seats to say goodbye.

They had come in out of the storm as strangers, and parted now as dear friends. "You'll be the best baitman on Deer Isle," Frank said in the ear of the young veteran who sat with closed eyes. He shook hands with Joshua Adams, and put another shiny penny in the toddler's fat little hand.

Delia patted the baby on the head and bent to give the tired young mother a kiss on the cheek. "Try to get some rest when you get home, dear," she whispered.

She gave the grandmother a hug. "You'll do well," she said. "I know you will."

Frank shook hands with the two men in plaid shirts. "I'll bet you hear from your son in just a few days," he said to the stout one.

When Frank shook hands with the fellow who'd fought in the Battle of the Wilderness, he received a vague smile in return. "You take good care of that dog," Frank said.

The brightness returned to the veteran's eyes. "I will," he said. "He'll be mighty glad to see me...start jumping up and licking my neck...." His face took on the satisfied smile that it had worn when he'd first joined the circle.

Cries of "Goodbye!" and "Good luck!" followed as Delia and Frank paused at the door to wave a last farewell. Tony led them to where a light double sleigh and a team of black horses waited. Delia carried her purse in the big bag Frank had brought from home, also her new hat with the crushed crown. She reflected that if it had happened a few days ago, she would have been upset. Now it seemed of small consequence.

Frank helped Delia into the sleigh, and she sandwiched herself between the two buffalo robes. Once settled, she looked about, trying to see as much as she could. Through the dwindling snow, she could see gangs of workmen, shoveling. "Everything is so white that Boston looks like a ghost town," she said to Frank.

The sleigh passed beneath tangled overhead wires. "Wind twists wires together," Tony said. "My brother, he knows to fix what's electric. He and other men work on the wires right now. He hears police say, 'Don't turn on power until you sure everything all right.'

"My cousin, Joe, he's a fireman. He says the mayor tells the fire chief, 'Have twenty-four extra horses ready, just in case.' Already one big house burns down."

"This is a strange time," Delia said. She pointed to a nearby building. "Look there! The snow has piled up so high it's almost to the tops of the doors."

"It'll take a lot of shoveling before anyone can get inside," Frank said.

Delia's cheeks had begun to burn in the icy cold, so she held her muff against her face for warmth. It also served as protection from the balls of hard packed snow that flew back into the sleigh from the horses's hooves.

"This isn't as bad a ride as I expected," Frank said to Tony. They were going down a wide main street where the snow had in many places been blown into heaps reaching from the center of the road to the fences or houses on one side, leaving the other side of the street for traffic.

Two men, one a doctor carrying his medical bag, waded through a drift as they approached a large house. The other must have gone to get him, Delia supposed. A woman wearing a long white apron stood in the doorway. A mid-wife, Delia thought immediately.

"Somebody's mighty sick, I guess," Frank said.

"Yes," Delia agreed. Perhaps a difficult birth, she said to herself, and shuddered. She'd seen too many deaths of young women—relatives and good friends. She wondered if men had any idea what women went through. Then she thought of Frank's sister, Cretia, saying Frank felt cheated because she hadn't been able to give him a son. Could his sister be right?

Two electric trains and a snowplow were stalled immediately ahead of them, blocking their way. Tony quickly changed directions, entering a street where there were so many drifts that there seemed no way to get through. Delia began to feel sick to her stomach as they went up and down, bumping over mountains of snow and sliding into valleys. Although Frank kept a tight arm around her, she wasn't sure if the next moment she would be still sitting between the buffalo robes on the sleigh or be bounced out into a snow bank.

The side street had its share of stalled vehicles, too. They passed abandoned milk wagons, bakery carts, and a buggy. The horses had been taken from the shafts and led to shelter.

On another street, Delia cried out, "Look at that new house, Frank. The builders hadn't put in the window glass yet, and the canvas that was over them is completely gone. I'm afraid the inside of the house is ruined."

She became suddenly aware of a tremendous drift immediately in front of them, and gave a shriek just before they drove through it. The horses came out the other side with their black backs painted white.

Delia was near tears as she tried to dig the snow out of the neck of her cape.

"Don't give up, Deal," Frank said. "We're at Atlantic Avenue now."

"Finally!" she said, shivering. As they passed the entrance way to several wharves, she caught glimpses of them, covered with dories and other small craft which had been torn from their moorings.

In many places the water had been forced well up onto the wide avenue, and when it receded left barrels, casks, planks...whatever hadn't been fastened down. The snow stopped, and they saw a gang of workmen, shoveling the debris from the roadway.

"Look there, Deal," Frank said, "the warehouse doors have been battered down and the ground floors flooded. Lots of losses."

"Atlantic Avenue didn't look like this last night, Frank, when we drove along it to India Wharf. Who could have imagined that all this would happen? Oh my! Look at those dead rats—ugly, ugly things!"

"They must have been washed out of their nests," Frank said.

"This morning, water all over these streets," Tony said. "Ground is low here. Big stable—bad flooded. Men go into it in rowboats. They find water up to the horses' necks."

"Good heavens, those poor animals," Delia said. And she wondered if their own two horses were all right.

They were at Eastern Avenue now, at the end of which sat the North Ferry, which they planned to take to East Boston.

Now with a clear view of the harbor, Delia and Frank were amazed at the sight of the beaches piled high with the wreckage of schooners and barges. She thought of the stout fellow in the plaid shirt, his son captain of a coal barge.

After Frank helped Delia down from the sleigh, he stood staring out over the water. He shook his head in disbelief. "Boston Harbor, famous as a safe-haven!"

"Frank," Delia said, tapping him on the arm to get his attention. "I'm going inside the ferry waiting room to get warm. You come along out of the cold when you can."

Inside, she saw only three other people, a North Ferry employee, wearing work clothes, and a well-dressed, middle-aged couple, standing near the stove, their backs to her.

"Why, if it isn't my good neighbors May Belle and Richard!" Delia exclaimed as she walked toward them. "I didn't see your horse and sleigh outside."

Richard, a short, sharp eyed man, chewing on a cigar, spoke out of the side of his mouth. "They're not here, Delia. The son-in-law just dropped us off."

"Oh, I'm so glad to see you," May Belle cried as she gave Delia a hug. "I thought you'd left for Maine on the *Portland*. I was worried sick thinking you were at sea."

"We missed the sailing," Delia said, "and decided to go by train. They weren't running, so we spent last night in North Station."

"Where's Frank?" Richard asked.

"He's outside staring at those wrecks in the harbor."

"A pitiful sight," Richard said. "It's been right nasty along the waterfront, Delia."

"You and Frank had no sooner left when our son-in-law came by to say our daughter was sick and needed us to take care of the children,"

May Belle said. "I put your cat out in the barn, where she could catch mice, and we left with Harold. We're just now going home."

Richard reached in his pocket for a handkerchief and blew his nose.

"He caught a terrible cold from being out in the heavy weather," May Belle said.

Richard cleared his throat. "My mate lives next door, and we started worrying about the fishing boat. 'Let's go down to the harbor and make sure it's still in one piece,' he said. I don't know how we did it, but in this morning's small hours we made it all the way from our daughter's down to Long Wharf."

"You didn't!" Delia exclaimed.

"We women begged them not to go," May Belle said.

Frank came in just then, still shaking his head in disbelief at the damage in the harbor. "Why, May Belle and Richard," he said, "what are you doing here?"

"We were at our daughter's," Richard told him. "My mate lives right next door. About two o'clock this morning, he and I got to worrying about the boat, and we made it from there down to Long Wharf."

"You didn't!"

"We did."

"I can hardly believe it," Frank said.

"We were desperate—we'd left the boat at anchor near the wharf, and we knew if she was gone, we were ruined."

"How did you manage to stay on your feet?" Frank asked.

"We held onto each other all the way down Atlantic Avenue, but that wind knocked us down again and again. The whole length of the avenue, and from there down to the deep water was strewn with a mass of wreckage. Barrels were in heaps or dashed to pieces."

Frank shook his head. "I can't believe you made it."

"After struggling along, a few feet at a time, we finally got there," Richard said. "The sea had ripped off the rafters and bumpers and thrown them about the wharf. The wharf itself was unsafe to walk on because a lot of the planks had been torn away, leaving great holes."

"So you started back," Frank said.

"No. Should have, if we'd had any sense. But right then the fear of poverty loomed stronger than the fear for our lives. We crawled down the lee side of the wharf and stared out into the harbor. A bad sight, I tell you. Huge waves rose high in the air and formed great whitecaps. The boat was nowhere in sight."

"I'm so sorry," Delia said. Her stormy vision, of the great liner that was breaking apart and the small schooner with the broken masts, returned unbidden to her mind.

"You're lucky to be alive, Mister," the workman said to Richard. "Last night two men off a five-masted schooner tried to reach their vessel in a small boat. The schooner was tossing and pulling at anchor a short distance out from the wharf. But the sea was running so swift, that they were forced to turn back. In the turning about, the younger fellow lost his life. The older one was rescued by a night watchman."

"A desperate time," Delia said.

"You four really need to get across this evening?" the workman asked.

"We do," Frank said, "also a young man with a sleigh and span of horses."

"I'll ask the captain if he'll make another run when the tide goes down a bit," the workman said. He stood up and began putting on his coat. "The tide is so high that the guards of the boats come above the piling of the ferry slips. We're afraid the ferries will catch there and be damaged."

"I can understand that," Frank said. "There's been more than enough damage already. That is one terrible mess out there."

The workman turned at the door. "Some people think about thirty men have been drowned or frozen to death right here in Boston Harbor. And I'd say about thirty-five vessels have been driven ashore or sunk." He walked out, closing the door behind him.

"What a sad time this is," May Belle said.

The workman returned rather quickly. "The captain says he'll make no more runs for awhile. The tide is too high to enter the slips with safety. He says to go down to the South Ferry—about a quarter of a mile from here. The slips are built higher there, and he expects the ferry will be operating."

Frank nodded, then turned to Delia. "We'd best do that. We can walk down there. I'll tell Tony to go home to his wife. We can't insist he stay with us. Maybe we can get a cab on the other side."

Richard wiped his nose. "I doubt you'll find one. The roads will be too bad. You're welcome to come to our son's, along with us, and stay the night. You know how close he lives to the ferry. I'll borrow a boat from someone, and we can go looking for mine in the morning."

"We appreciate your offer to stay at your son's," Frank said. "But if possible, we'd like to get home now, look after the horses, and make sure everything is all right. We'll check your place, too. Then I'll come back at first light to help you hunt."

"I appreciate your checking on the horses," May Belle said. "Richard asked the boy across the street to look after them, but I don't think he's very reliable."

Richard wiped his nose again. "If we don't find my boat...well, I do have some insurance, but not enough to buy another one."

Frank left to talk to Tony. He found the young man walking back and forth, watching the horses, which were now covered with blankets. Tony was clapping his hands against his legs to keep his blood circulating.

After Frank spoke to him about leaving, Tony said, "You need me. I need money. We start for other ferry."

"All right, then," Frank said, "I'll tell my wife."

Delia stood just inside the door, waiting. Frank had barely stepped inside before she asked, "Is he leaving now?"

"No. Tony says he'll go down to the South Ferry with us. But I'm going outside to watch the horses, while he comes inside for a bit to get warm."

"I'm glad he'll see us home, Frank."

"So far it's been a slow day for me," the workman commented. "The ferry has run just a few times. You wouldn't believe the tides. I found a difference of about 16 and a half feet between high and low water."

"It sounds like the tides around St. John, where I grew up," Delia said.

"The Bay of Fundy," the workman said, "highest tides in the world. By the way," he added, grinning, "those toll takers on the East Boston side were mad as Hades earlier today, before noon. The waiting rooms were flooded from seven to eight inches, the water even going into the toll takers' houses. They were marooned there on their stools till the tide went down."

Because of the discomfort from the cold, the South Ferry seemed farther than the quarter of a mile the workman had said it was. When they arrived, the boat stood ready to leave. As they climbed aboard, the ferry swayed, lifted, and fell with the moving water. As the horses whinnied with fear, Tony and Frank held onto their halters so they wouldn't rear up.

Delia, May Belle and Richard went inside. Several others were there before them, looking out the windows at the sorry scene in the harbor.

"I had a family member at sea when the gale struck," an elderly woman said. "My niece was going Down East to marry a salt water farmer. I don't suppose I have to worry, though, not with her aboard a fine vessel like the *Portland*."

Richard wiped his nose with his soggy handkerchief. "I imagine Captain Blanchard put into Gloucester, when the weather got too heavy."

"It's the only anchorage he could make after leaving Boston," another man said, then turned to smile reassuringly at the woman. "That sidewheeler is a beauty of a ship, and Blanchard wouldn't take any chances with her."

Delia didn't know why, but she suddenly had the thought that the big ship seen so hazily in her vision might have been the *Portland*. No, what a crazy idea ...not a well-made ship like that, built less than ten years ago!

The water was becoming so rough she felt sick to her stomach. Snow was falling again.

Once on the East Boston shore, Richard, in between sniffing and sneezing, said in a hoarse voice to Frank, "I'll borrow a boat and be ready to go in the morning. I hope the seas are calmer." Then he and May Belle started walking toward their son's house.

When Tony had hitched the horses to the sleigh, Delia, Frank and Tony got into it and started off on a shore road that had been water swept, so was free of snow banks. The men got out several times to move trees that had blown down.

If we get home tonight, it will be a miracle, Delia thought. When they finally approached their house, she felt her heart pounding with anxiety.

"Oh dear!" she exclaimed when they came within sight of it. "Look at our beautiful big silver poplar—uprooted! And the house, Frank—most of the shutters are torn off—and the walls—they're absolutely crusted with ice and snow."

"The weathervane's gone from the barn," Frank said, "and some of the shingles ripped off the roof. Sure hope the horses are alive."

A path had been shoveled to the barn, and Delia knew that her brother George had been there.

Frank made his way up the path, opened the door, then turned to shout, "There's been flooding, but both horses are all right!"

"Wonderful!" Delia called back.

Meanwhile, Tony had shoveled a path to the house and cleaned off the porch steps.

Frank walked back along the path to the house, and with some difficulty turned the big key in the lock which was stiff from the cold. "You come in for a cup of hot coffee and some of my wife's fruitcake," he said to Tony.

"I think I can't wait for coffee. If I take too long, my Rose worries too much. But cake is good."

As Delia cut several big pieces, Frank reached in his pocket and gave him seven dollars.

"As much as I get in a week," Tony said. "Rose will be happy."

"Best of luck with the baby," Frank said heartily.

Did Frank feel, as she sometimes did, that everyone but them had children? She wouldn't have minded not having them, but perhaps his sister Cretia was right. Maybe a son was what he wanted more than anything in the world.

While Frank went to check on May Belle's and Richard's place, she got the coal stove going, then made tea for herself, coffee for Frank, and cut some more wedges of fruitcake, all the while trying to get up the courage to ask him.

"Their horses are all right, and their house looks about like ours, Deal," he said as he came back inside, stomping the snow from his boots on the rug by the door. "Tomorrow I'll send a telegram to Eph. He and Euda and Cretia will be worried when we don't show up."

After he sat down at the table, he added an afterthought. "He won't get it right away though, with the wires down. Western Union will do the first repairs in cities, but as small as Pemaquid Harbor is, it'll be left till last. Might even be a couple of weeks. Why don't you write a letter, Deal? It will get there faster."

"I will," she said.

As she put the coffee and fruitcake before him, he nodded his appreciation. "I don't know if you noticed, Deal, but I gave Tony the 50 cent pieces I was going to give the young folks in Maine."

"It was the right thing to do," Delia said. She thought of how Frank loved being with young people: how he enjoyed going fishing with his nephews, the kindness he'd shown Tony, and to the fellow who'd lost his leg in the war. They might have been the ages of his own sons, if she'd been able to give him children.

"Frank," she began in her whispery voice, "do you ever feel cheated, Frank, not to have children...not to have a son? Your sisters think you feel that way." Her hand was shaking so hard she didn't dare pick up the cup of tea for fear of spilling it.

He looked surprised. "My sisters said that? What do they know about the way I feel? Do I ever feel cheated? No. Not for a moment."

"But Frank, we used to talk about having children. We even picked out names, remember?"

"I tried to go along with what I thought you wanted, Deal, even if it wasn't what I wanted. I've seen what happens when children come along. They get all the woman's attention, and the husband is out in the cold."

"You really feel that way, Frank?"

He reached across the table and took both her hands in his. "I do."

After a moment, a smile crossed his bearded lips. "You know how a lot of times, after church, couples have come up to us to brag about a son who's doing well? They seem to be very happy, but I've noticed that as they talk, the men's eyes are on you, not on their own lumpy wives. Don't I know that those fellows would give up everything to have a woman like you?"

"Oh, Frank," she said through happy tears. "Oh Frank...."

"I never wanted anything but you, Deal."

Chapter 14

The Day the Mail Came

Joe and Zena

In the icy cold kitchen, Zena, in her crocheted slippers, and heavy outdoor jacket over her long flannel nightgown, prepared the fire in the woodstove. She sprinkled kerosene over the kindling, put a match to it, and as the fire took hold, quickly put the iron cover back in place.

The wind was quieter now, as though worn out from a terrible tantrum.

"The storm should stop soon," Joe said from the bedroom, as he got dressed. "Have to start shoveling the road. Mail carrier's got to get through with the newspapers. Got to make sure the boys' vessels aren't wrecked or lost. Can't rest till we find out."

They'd been awake most of the night. Sometimes when the worry about their boys became an almost overwhelming pain, one of them would reach for the comfort of the other's hand.

From time to time Joe would say, "Them boys are all right, Zena."

Thinking the fear she felt might be heard in her voice, she said nothing, but gave his hand a squeeze.

When Joe came through the bedroom door into the kitchen, he had on his heavy wool pants and two flannel shirts.

"Soon as the stove heats up, I'll fix you some griddle cakes." she said.

"Can't wait." He sat on the deacon's bench in front of the fireplace and began pulling on his boots, then stood by the stove and gulped down a cup of cold coffee. "It's still coming down, but I can make a start."

After he'd put on his fearnaught, hat, gloves and muffler, she stuck a couple of slices of napkin-wrapped brown bread in his pocket, then pulled the muffler up over his mouth and nose to prevent frostbite.

She watched from the window as shovel in hand he walked and slid over the ice covered snow. The drifts were so high, ten feet or more, that the only clue to the whereabouts of the road were a couple of broken-off telegraph poles.

She heard Josie get up from the cot in the birthing room. She'd spent the night there so Zena could watch over her. In the early hours of the morning Zena had heard the girl's breath come easier.

"You're looking better, Josie," she said, as her daughter came into the kitchen blowing her nose. "You grease yourself up once more, and that should do it." She lifted a small pan from the back of the stove.

"I hate that stuff," Josie said, but began unbuttoning the neck of her nightgown as she walked back toward the birthing room with the goose grease.

"I've made some elderberry tea for you. It will heat up soon. The fire on the hearth has taken hold now, so you sit there and keep warm. Your father is shoveling, and I'm going out to feed the stock and do the milking."

Zena dressed quickly. Before going out to the barn, she made fresh coffee, then went to the window, to see if by chance the snow had grown so light that she could see Joe. She saw him not far from the window leaning on his shovel. He hadn't even reached the road. One hand was pressed over the closed eyelid, where the cancerous eye had been, and she knew he was in pain. She would shovel as soon as she could.

Outdoors, she hurried in the direction of the barn. As she pushed back the door, the young horse whinnied a greeting from his stall. Today, however, with her mind on the boys at sea, she hadn't thought to bring him pieces of apple in her apron pocket. As the cows ate from their troughs, Zena milked them, and then struggled into the house with the heavy pails.

"I ought to be out helping father shovel," Josie said.

"Stay inside until you get better. You know how easily you get pneumonia." She strained the warm liquid through cheesecloth into shallow pans, set them in the cellar way to cool, then hurried to the window to signal she was coming to help shovel.

But Joe, looking spent and cold, was walking up toward the house. She quickly lit the oven, cut a generous piece of mince pie, and stuck it in to warm. The hearty filling of meat, apples, brown sugar, raisins and currents would "stick to his ribs," as her mother used to say. She reached to the top shelf for his cup, which she filled with hot coffee.

He stamped off most of the snow onto the small braided rug inside the door, pulled out a straight backed chair from around the table, and dropped into it. After a few minutes, he began struggling, with cold-stiffened fingers, to take off his boots. Zena bent to pull them off.

"Them mountains and pyramids kept me from seeing up toward Scotty or down toward Pemaquid," he said.

Turning his chair to face the table, he took a forkful of the pie Zena brought him, then a sip of the nearly boiling coffee. "Haven't been able to see any neighbors yet—know they're shoveling, though. Everybody's wanting to see the papers."

"Everybody wants to, but everybody's afraid to," Josie said.

"Ayuh," he said,—"about right."

He took another sip of the steaming coffee. "No chance of getting them drifts between here and Bristol Road leveled today, but we've got to keep at it."

Late Tuesday afternoon, when Zena was shoveling by herself, she managed to scoop off part of a 12-foot drift, and caught sight of a neighbor up the road, shoveling hard. They waved and exchanged "halloos," then returned to work. She was beginning to tire now, and her heart beat so fast she knew she had to stop. Joe, watching from the window, came out to take the shovel and work until dark.

"We're getting some place now, Zena," he said that evening as he ate his salt codfish hash and biscuits.

"Thank God for that, Joe."

The next day, after the morning chores were done, Zena went down to the road to help Joe shovel. After about an hour and a half, both were overcome with exhaustion. They had stopped to lean on their shovels, when a neighbor from up the road pointed and shouted, "Look there!"

Joe and Zena turned and saw in the distance three teams of horses coming from the direction of four corners, where the township offices were. They were pulling a heavy roller the width of the road. Zena and Joe looked at each other through tears of relief. Help was on the way!

By noon the snow had been packed hard all the way up to Bristol Road. The mail carrier could get through. Thank the Lord!

That afternoon, all of the village men were at the post office, waiting. They didn't do much talking, mostly just smoked their pipes and whittled.

When the mail carrier pulled up outside in his sleigh, the men rose to their feet in anticipation. Joe opened the door.

Although the carrier usually talked a blue streak, bringing the latest funny stories he'd collected along the route, he was silent today. Without more than a nod to the group, he dropped the heavy mailbag from his shoulder onto the rough floor boards.

The waiting men stood completely silent now. Then Joe, who couldn't stand the suspense, asked in a voice that cracked, "Is the news bad?"

The fellow moved his quid of tobacco to the side of his mouth. "Lots of losses. Steamer *Portland* wrecked off Highland Light—34 bodies washed up so far."

"Oh Lord! Frank and Delia."

A neighbor put a hand on Joe's shoulder. "There might be survivors."

Another added, "That's right—might have been picked up by a passing steamer."

The neighbors lined up, waiting for postmaster Henry Goudy to sort the mail. He worked quickly, and within a few minutes all were served. A young lobsterman with a *Kennebec Journal*, lowered his paper, and looked at Joe who stared at the front page of the *Boston Globe*.

The fellow gave a small cough to get Joe's attention. "A notice here about the *Addie E.*" He held up the page and pointed to the section headed

TWENTY-SEVEN VESSELS WRECKED.

"Can't seem to read it," Joe said, as the words blurred in front of his eyes.

"It says, 'The coaster Addie E. Snow of Rockland, Me. drifted ashore at Race Point this afternoon.' That's all."

Joe nodded, his lips pressed tightly together, his eyes glazed. He stumbled out the door, carrying the several days worth of the *Lewiston Evening Journal* and the *Boston Globe.* The young man followed him outside and put his paper on top of Joe's. "Mrs. Brown and Josie might want to see this."

As Joe walked slowly up the rise of the yard, Zena and Josie stood at the kitchen window, their faces tense. When he was only half way there, Zena opened the door. "Any news?" she shouted.

He nodded, without speaking. On the way home, he had stacked the newspapers according to date, then debated with himself, as to which bad news he should let them know first. After he stepped inside, he put his Lewiston and Boston papers into the rocker, but held onto the "Kennebec Journal."

Zena's nerves were at the breaking point. "Well, what did you learn, Joe?"

Holding her by the arm, he pointed to the sentence about the *Addie E. Snow.*

After she read it, her legs gave way, and she would have fallen if Joe hadn't had hold of her arm. He and Josie helped her to the deacon's bench. After a minute Zena looked up with tears in her eyes. "It doesn't say, Joe. It doesn't say if the men were saved."

Josie picked up the paper and read where her father pointed with a shaking hand. "Race Point," she said tearfully. "Drifted ashore at Race Point."

They all knew about that place—the farthest point on east Cape Cod. The boys had spoken of it often—about its shifting sands, and its weathered gray dune shacks made of driftwood from shipwrecks.

"Does the *Boston Globe* say anything about the *Addie E.?*" Zena whispered.

"Not about the *Addie E.*, but...." He carefully picked out the Monday paper and placed it in her hands. It was best not to let her know the worst right away.

She looked at the front page and gasped. "The *Portland*—it says here she didn't come into port on Sunday—oh my! Frank and Delia!"

"The steamer must have waited out the storm in a safe harbor," Josie said. She picked up the following day's *Lewiston Evening Journal*, and read the headlines aloud.

"SEARCH BEGUN. TWO CUTTERS DISPATCHED TO FIND
THE PORTLAND. MISSING STEAMER WAS NOT SIGHTED
BY SISTER SHIPS."

"Probably the next day's paper will say where they found her." Josie reached for it, looked at the front page, and began to cry. "Oh no! No!"

"What is it, Josie?" Zena asked, leaning forward.

"It says—it says the *Portland* sank," she whispered.

"It can't be true!" Zena moaned. "I can't believe it!"

"My beautiful Aunt Delia—my beautiful Aunt Delia and my wonderful Uncle Frank!" Josie sobbed, sinking onto the bench beside her mother.

Joe, who had been standing by the window looking out at the endless snow, the broken trees and telegraph poles, turned, and said in an expressionless voice, "They might have been picked up by another ship."

"Yes," Josie said. "That's what I'm going to believe. It happened to Lemmie when he was shipwrecked off Delaware, and it happened to Uncle Frank when he was cast ashore on Goodwin Sands." Sniffing and wiping her eyes, she added, "I'm going to have faith they were saved."

"Yes," Zena, said in a hollow voice. "We've got to have faith." She stood up and began walking aimlessly about the kitchen, then sat down again.

"I bet there's something on the inside pages that tells about a rescue ship," Josie said.

Zena glanced down at the paper as Josie turned the page, and saw in large print, "LIST OF VICTIMS." She began to tremble. After a couple of minutes, she took a deep breath, and said, "Read down the list, Josie."

The girl swallowed hard, and began running her finger down the page looking for "Stevens." "Here! No, that's a Stevens from Woodford." She stood up and began pacing back and forth across the kitchen, as she continued her search. "Their names aren't in here," she said. "I knew they wouldn't be."

Zena, too exhausted from emotion to talk, signalled to Joe that she wanted him to bring her the rest of the papers. The headline of the one she picked up read:

"LIST OF PORTLAND'S VICTIMS GROWS HOUR BY HOUR,
AS RELATIVES COME FORWARD."

The story beneath said the only passenger list had gone down with the ship. It gave no hope of any survivors.

Zena put her hands over her face and rocked back and forth on the bench. "It's my punishment for being unforgiving and self-righteous. If only I could put my arms around Frank and Delia and tell them I loved them. I didn't have any special cure for spinal meningitis. Why did I make myself believe that if Frank had telegraphed earlier, I could have saved May?"

Joe sat down beside her, and held her tight. She began to weep on his shoulder.

He gently stroked her hair. "You couldn't stand losing her, Zena. Had to blame someone—had to." After awhile Zena, drained of emotion, sat up straight, wiped her eyes on Joe's handkerchief, and said in a flat voice, "I'd better fix supper." In a daze, she stirred up some griddle cakes, but no one could eat.

Early Thursday afternoon Joe went to wait in the little post office. Others followed, until the place was full, and they had to stand close to make room for the mail carrier when he came in.

When Joe got his mail, he began, with shaking hands, to leaf through the "Lewiston Evening Journal." He was looking up one column and down another, when under the section headed "Memoranda" the name *Addie E. Snow* leaped out at him: "Schooner Addie E. Snow of Rockland came ashore at Race Point and is a total loss."

"A total loss?" Joe said, unaware he was speaking out loud. "Oh Lord, what does that mean for our boy?"

There were sympathetic murmurs and pats on the shoulder, as one by one the others left the post office. He walked slowly home.

"Any news about Percy?" Zena asked in a quiet voice, as he opened the kitchen door.

"Same as yesterday, but today they added that the vessel is a total loss. Still no news about the men. He showed the sentence to Zena.

"Let me see," Josie said, and he handed her the paper. After a minute she gasped, "Look here—at the other side of the page! A report about Race Point life saving station and the *Addie E. Snow*!"

She began reading fast—out loud. "'Captain Clark and his men had rescued a part of the crew of the Bucksport schooner Addie E. Snow, which had gone ashore at this point Sunday forenoon about nine o'clock. He told the Press reporter the story of the rescue.

"'The wind was blowing so hard you couldn't stand up and face it,' said Captain Clark. 'We saw the schooner coming a long way off and knew that she would go onto the bar.'"

"Oh Lord," Joe said. "Oh Lord!"

"'We had to shovel sand for fifteen or twenty minutes before we could get the door of our houses open so as to get out any of our apparatus. We finally succeeded in getting out a little practice gun and with this we went down under the bluffs to a point opposite to where the schooner was coming ashore. She struck about as soon as we got there. A man could not stand up and face the wind. The sand cut the faces of the men so that the blood rolled off their cheeks.

"'Two men were swept off the schooner's poop as soon as she struck and a sea took them around under her bow toward us.'"

"Do you think one was Percy?" Josie asked.

"I hope," Joe said. "Might have a good chance from there."

Josie's hands began shaking so hard that she couldn't hold the paper steady, but she went on reading. "'This wave landed them at the top of the bluff thirty feet high and the men grabbed and scratched to hold on to keep from being swept back into the sea. We grabbed him and pulled him in behind the bluff where he sank down exhausted.'"

"What happened to the other poor critter?" Joe cried.

Josie shook her head and continued reading at a rapid rate.

"'Then we fired a shot over the schooner's mizzen crosstrees. There were four men on this mast, but none of them touched this rope which was within reach of them all. Finally one man did take hold of the rope and started to pull in the larger rope. He pulled away alone but no one offered to help him. At last he got the big rope with the breeches buoy attached and made it fast. Then we pulled him in.'"

Josie paused long enough to cry, "Oh, I hope that was Percy!"

"'Another man tried to come ashore on the rope and was snatched off by the sea. The two men who were left then made an attempt together to come in over the line. They were so frightened that they did not understand how to work the breeches buoy. They got on the line and it began to surge and sag. We held on for dear life on the other end, but suddenly the mast went by the board and the two men were swept out to sea.'"

Josie took a deep breath, and read on in a shaky voice.

"'These four men which the reporter understood Captain Clark had saved were given as follows: Raymond Sprague, Machias; R.F. Jones, Boston; Frank N. Woods, Glasgow; John Ellegard, Denmark.'"

Josie burst our crying. "It doesn't say Percy! It doesn't say Percy!"

Zena got up abruptly and put her arms around her daughter. "No Josie, the newspaper's all mixed up. She wasn't Percy's schooner. This was a big vessel with a lot of men on her. The *Addie E.* had just five,—all from around Rockland."

"I noticed they called her a Bucksport schooner," Joe said quietly, his face drained of color. "I figured they just got their towns mixed up....Oh Lord, them poor critters who were washed out to sea...."

Josie dabbed at her tears and looked further down the column. "Now the reporter is telling what Captain Clark says about the wreckage from the *Portland*," she said in a hushed voice. "'At eleven forty-five a surf man came in to the house and reported that wreckage of various kinds was coming ashore fast. We got out our crew and went down along the beach. Not a thing could be seen or heard excepting the roar of the surf. We did not find any bodies there until the next forenoon about eight or nine o'clock. The first body that came ashore was up near high head station. This was the body of a woman with a cut on her head. Soon after this we got two more bodies along this station."

"Poor souls," Zena said, and added in an undertone, "I hope to God that one of them wasn't Delia."

Josie read at a desperate rate. "'Several bodies were sighted in the surf some distance from shore, but they disappeared from view in the strong current running southward, and it was impossible to get hold of them. The majority were carried down the coast toward Monomoy and Nantucket. Many old mariners predict that a large number of bodies will never be recovered.'

"I can't read anymore," Josie said. "It's too sad." She dropped the paper onto her mother's lap, then ran out of the kitchen and up the steep narrow stairs to her bedroom.

Chapter 15

Losses

Hattie Belle, in an oversized flower print apron over an indigo-blue dress, stood at the iron sink, trimming the kerosene lamps. As she cleaned the greasy glass chimneys, she listened for the creak of the side door. Her father had gone for the mail, and she hoped the newspapers he brought back would have good reports about Lemmie's ship, the *Scorpion*.

The big window behind the sink revealed a cold grey sky above an ice and snow covered world. In the near backyard, most of the branches of the apple trees, their pink and white blossoms always lovely in spring, had been broken off by the storm. She caught sight of a thin red fox chasing a snowshoe rabbit.

Mary, in a brown wrapper with a ruffle at the hem, laid out ingredients for making the ginger cookies requested by Captain Davis. The two women didn't talk. They waited for him to come home with the newspapers' life or death news. After yesterday's statement in the *Lincoln County News*, reporting that all contact with the gunboat *Scorpion* had been lost, Hattie Belle feared it meant the ship had gone down.

"In heavy weather, ships can be blown off course, then found some time later," Captain Davis said.

She had to know what had happened to the *Scorpion*, yet didn't know as she could stand it if the news was bad. When she heard the hall door open, she ran toward it, drying her hands on her apron. "What do the papers say about Lemmie's ship?" she cried.

He held out a thick letter. "From your young man, himself. Now you can stop worrying."

"Oh, thank God!" Hattie Belle said, tears coming to her eyes. She held it over her heart as she rushed into the next room and closed the door behind her. Alone by the fireplace, she savored each word. The long letter was full of plans for their future. From time to time she stopped to dab at her eyes. All their dreams were about to come true.

A friend of Lemmie's mother, who lives in Clark's Cove, had written to tell him the cottage with the lilacs around it would be for rent at the first of the year; and the friend had finagled a job for him—cutting ice for the rest of the winter. The next wonderful piece of news had came from a letter sent by the I.L.Snow Company. They promised that come spring he could be master of one of their lime schooners, and his bride could sail with him.

Lemmie ended his letter by saying he had to be the happiest man alive. On another piece of paper, he had written in a hurried scrawl, "A fellow who owns a sugar plantation gave me a parrot called Jocko. The bird swears like a pirate, but all in Spanish, so the preacher won't be shocked when he comes calling."

Smiling through happy tears, Hattie Belle left the warmth of the fireplace and opened the door to the kitchen, intending to share some of the good news. Her father sat at the table with Mary, newspaper pages spread out in front of him, his face grim.

"I have some bad news," Captain Davis said, and he held up the front page of a newspaper.

NOT ONE SAVED

The steamer Portland Lost With All On Board Sunday Morning.

Driven Clear Across Massachusetts Bay in the Fierce Gale.

Struck on Peaked Hill Bar and Went to Pieces.

Bodies of the Victims Washed Ashore Near Provincetown.

"Delia and Frank Stevens!" Hattie Belle cried.

Mary wiped her eyes.

The thought of their bodies washing up on shore hit Hattie Belle so hard she couldn't even cry. She remembered the last time she'd seen them—at the Wednesday night prayer meeting before they'd returned to East Boston. Delia had been even more beautiful than usual in a green and lavender organdy gown, with a lovely gold brooch at the neck; and he had been handsome in a light grey summer suit and a high collared white shirt.

"Do you think there is a chance Frank and Delia might be alive, Will?" Mary asked.

"It's almost beyond hope. Might be that a person tied to a plank could survive, but I doubt it."

"Maybe a steamship bound for Europe took off some of those aboard the *Portland*," Hattie Belle ventured. She picked up another newspaper, also with headlines about the *Portland*, and began hunting for the shipping news, to find the names of vessels recently bound for Europe. As she turned the pages, a familiar name in a list of wrecked vessels leaped out at her: "The Addie E. Snow washed ashore at Race Point." Feeling sick to her stomach, she held out the page to her father, and pointed to the name of Percy's schooner. Her worried eyes held an unspoken question.

He shook his head gravely. "Can't tell by this if the men were saved or not. Doesn't seem too long ago that Zena and Joe's oldest boy, Frank, was lost in an ice storm off Barnegat Bay."

Not lost like Frank, Hattie Belle thought. Not lost like Frank. Overcome with emotion, she stood facing the window so they couldn't see she was crying. Is Percy gone now, too? she asked herself. Is it true what some people say, that there is a curse on the Brown family? Its import frightened her.

With great effort she brought herself back to the present moment, and looked down the long yard that sloped to the water. The tree branches were covered with ice, and a mountain of snow had piled up along the stone wall. That was where she had sat on a spring day, two and a half years ago, when Lemmie had come back from Russia with a ruby ring.

Down beyond the stone wall, at the path's end, wrecked vessels lay on the rocks. Two lobstermen were picking up pieces of their boats.

"I've found a long list of schooners and steamships destroyed in the gale," Captain Davis said. "I'm afraid I see some familiar names."

I don't want to hear them, she thought, as the horror of the *Portland's* sinking came rushing back.

Captain Davis motioned her over to the table, and she stood looking over his shoulder at the headlines above the article.

COAST STREWN WITH WRECKS.

Dreadful Destruction of Shipping During the Fearful Blizzard.

From All Points Come Reports of Disaster With Loss of Life.

Many Maine Vessels Included in the Long and Growing List.

"Sit down," he said. "I hate to say it, but most likely a number of wrecked vessels weren't found or identified when this was written."

She reluctantly pulled out a chair. "If you find the name of Lawrence's schooner, the *Robert A. Snow*, or any bad news about the crew of the *Addie E. Snow*, I don't believe I can stand to hear it."

"It won't help to put off the knowing," Captain Davis said, and began reading aloud: "'There was a terrible scene here at Thompson's Island.'"

I know just where it is in Boston Harbor, Hattie Belle wanted to scream, and I don't want to hear about it.

Captain Davis was reading about the death of his friend, Captain Jonas Israel. "A good man," he said, when finished, and passed a hand across his eyes. "You must remember him, Hattie Belle, from the days I used to take you to Boston with me."

"I do," she said, and pulled aside her apron to reach into the pocket of her dress for a handkerchief. Those were the summers after Mama died, she remembered.

"It says one person from that vessel was saved, the captain's son, 'who was washed ashore and was resuscitated.' We've got to be thankful for that. If it was the father's life for the son's, it's what my friend would have wanted."

He paused, a worried frown between his eyes, then went on with his reading. "'Four down east vessels, anchored far from each other, were brought up against a pier. Barely a vestige is left of the *Virginia*. The other vessels are the *Watchman* the *Seraphine* and the *Fred M. Emerson*.' The paper says the last three vessels are a heap of timber and rigging mixed with debris from the *Virginia*. Terrible!

"I reckon I'd better read on. Schooner *Lucy Belle* is totally wrecked. She was sailing from Sullivan, Maine, for Dorchester, and is ashore in South Cove, Boston harbor. I've seen that vessel many a time."

Hattie Belle tried not to listen. How she would get through this day and those that followed, she didn't know. Perhaps a person could endure hearing one day's tragedies. But her father believed not all the wrecked vessels had been found or identified. It meant tomorrow, and on the days following, more people would be listed as lost. It would be like an unending funeral.

"Please don't read out loud any more, Papa," Hattie Belle said. "I can't bear it."

Mary got up and walked over to the work table. "I don't want to hear anymore either. The sinking of the *Portland* and the deaths of Delia and Frank are tragedy enough." Although she was a precise person who liked to measure ingredients carefully, today she began throwing everything helter skelter into a big white enamel bowl: molasses, brown sugar, lard, ginger, saleratus, salt and flour. She added boiling water from the kettle, and beat the dough with strong angry strokes. "Is it any wonder that I hate the sea?" she snapped. Suddenly she turned away from the work table. "I don't feel well," she said.

"Sorry," Captain Davis said. "Take one of your headache powders and lie down for awhile."

Mary took the medicine with some water and started toward the dining-living room, then half-turned. "If the batter is any good, you can bake some cookies, Hattie Belle. If not, give it to the hens." And she left, closing the door behind her.

Hattie Belle floured the bread board and rolled out the dough. She hadn't taken a taste of Mary's mixture. But whether it was good or bad didn't matter. Right now, working with it, cutting out the cookies, and greasing the baking sheets gave her something to do. After awhile she began crying softly to herself, as she thought of Percy's vessel, washed ashore at Race Point. She prayed that he still lived.

Captain Davis continued to read under his breath the list of vessels known to be lost and the list of their dead, stopping now and then to cry out, "Sunk with all her crew!"

As the cookies were baking, Hattie Belle stood in front of the kitchen window where one could look down over harbor rocks covered with broken boats. After she pulled the last batch of ginger cookies from the oven, she walked back to the window again, and thought of the way the harbor looked in summer, its dark blue water sparkling in the sunshine. The boarders, as they sat on the porch, and ate strawberries and cream, would watch endlessly. They never tired of its charms. How little they knew of the water's savage moods in winter, or the terrors and tragedies it could bring.

She studied the shore directly across the harbor, noting its broken wharves and damaged cottages. Her face brushed against the old plant hanging in the kitchen window, a Wandering Jew. It was the last one of her mother's that still lived. As she poured it a drink from a watering pot, she saw out of the corner of her eye that a sleigh carrying two people was turning onto their road. Who could they be, to come visiting on a day this cold, and over such rough roads?

She ran to look out the hall window at the visitors. "It's Ella, and Ozias," she called back to her father, "Lemmie's cousins." Poor little Ella, at fourteen, she spent her days doing housework and taking care of her mother, who was so crippled with arthritis she was like a living statue.

Because good manners had been instilled in Hattie Belle at an early age, and they included looking well groomed when company arrived, she hurried to the kitchen looking glass near the sink to see if her reflection proved her presentable. She wiped a bit of cookie dough off her cheek and fluffed the sides of her hair with her fingers. When she took off her apron, she was relieved to see a spotless dress.

Captain Davis folded his newspapers and put them under the small table by his rocking chair. "I guess I've read all that I can stand to know about wrecked Maine ships and lost friends." He reached for his hat and coat behind the door. "I'll go help get the horse into the barn."

The coffee and tea were already made, so all she needed to do was to fill a plate with the still-warm ginger cookies—after tasting a few crumbs to make sure they were edible. She took cups and saucers from the china cabinet.

Hattie Belle had placed the plate of cookies on the starched white tablecloth, when a terrifying reason for the visit hit her so hard it took her strength, and she had to sit down in one of the oak chairs that lined the kitchen table.

Ella and Ozias wouldn't have come all the way over from the John's River side of the peninsula on a day like this, unless something had happened to Lemmie. Could one of their newspapers have something dreadful in it about the *Scorpion*? On legs that could hardly carry her, Hattie Belle walked down the short hall, which now seemed so long she wasn't sure she could get to the end. She must mind her manners—call out a greeting. When she opened the door, she saw that Ella was just a few yards away, hurrying along the shoveled path, holding her long wool cloak away from the banks of snow at either side.

Hattie Belle opened her mouth to say, "It's good to see you, Ella," but fear had taken her breath away, and nothing came out but a faint whisper.

She heard Ozias call "Hello, Hattie!" and she managed to wave in return. Now eighteen, and a lobsterman, he looked so much like Lemmie, with his dark moustache and curly hair showing from beneath the edge of his stocking cap, her eyes started to fill with tears. But she blinked them back.

"It's good to be in out of the cold," Ella said, as Hattie Belle took her wraps and hung them behind the door. The girl pushed a stray lock of thick black hair, away from her face. "I don't look very nice. My father made me wear a couple of his wool shirts."

"You look fine. Just right for such weather."

When they were seated at the kitchen table, each with a cup of hot tea in her hand, and the plate of ginger cookies in front of them, Ella said, "Uncle Eph's family and Aunt Cretia's are at our house now. They've brought their newspapers with them, and they're trying to piece together the different reports to find out what happened to Uncle Frank and Aunt Delia, and Percy, and Lawrence. They fear the worst. Mother has cried until she is almost sick, and her rheumatiz hurts her worse than ever.

"I'm sorry," Hattie Belle murmured.

"Uncle Eph thinks with our three families all taking different newspapers, we must know more about the storm than anyone around. He said because you will so soon be a part of our family, he wanted you to know what we've been able to figure out."

Hattie Belle's cup, with its blue lovebirds soaring over a China sea, trembled in her hand. She managed to return it to the saucer, without spilling any of the tea on the tablecloth. Have you found out something about Lemmie? she wanted to ask. Isn't that the real reason you came? Did one of the newspapers say the *Scorpion* sank?

"Have you heard that my Uncle Frank and Aunt Delia had tickets for the *Portland* Saturday night?"

Hattie Belle nodded. "Your Aunt Cretia told my stepmother."

Ella fiddled with a button on a cuff of her black and white checked shirt, and Hattie Belle noticed that her fingers were cracked and red from scrubbing the family's clothes on the wash board. The girl seemed to be getting herself ready to tell something she didn't want to talk about.

"Uncle Eph has said, ever since the storm, that there must have been red flags flying in Boston the way they were in Damariscotta, so he felt sure that Uncle Frank and Aunt Delia would have decided to come by train. He figured they'd stay in Newcastle or Damariscotta, then come along by stage as soon as the roads were passable."

She took a deep breath. "Uncle Eph met the stage today...but they weren't on it. I asked him if there was a chance that another vessel might have rescued them from the sinking *Portland*. 'I suppose it's possible,' he said, but we could tell by the sound of his voice and the look in his eye that he didn't believe it was."

Hattie Belle, wiped away tears with her napkin.

Ella took her handkerchief out of her reticule, unfolded and refolded it. "Have you read about Percy's schooner being washed ashore at Race Point?"

"I have, but I'm clinging to the hope that the men were saved." She stared out the window at the snow-covered world, seeing in her mind's eye a small schooner thrown up onto the dunes by an angry sea.

The girl shifted in her chair. "Have you read anything about Lawrence's schooner, the *Robert A. Snow*?"

Startled, Hattie Belle looked quickly toward her. "No. No, I haven't." Lawrence mustn't be lost—not Lawrence. It would be almost as bad as losing Lemmie. When you saw them together they were so exactly alike they seemed, somehow, to be a part of each other. Then she thought of Myrtie Belle. Why, she and Lawrence were still on their honeymoon—just beginning their new life together.

"All of us are afraid for them," Ella said. "Last week my folks got a thank you letter from Lawrence for the wedding gift they'd sent. He wrote that he was in New York, and planned to leave the next day for Salem harbor. From the date on the letter, Uncle Eph figured back the days, and the time it would take Lawrence to make the run, and said the *Robert A.*

would have reached Salem in plenty of time before the heavy weather started."

She took a deep breath. "I'll try to remember just what Monday's Lewiston paper said about that port." She closed her eyes, trying to repeat the exact wording— "Up to six o'clock the worst shipping disaster reported was the wrecking of nine vessels of the coasting fleet in Salem harbor."

Quietly, they both began to cry. After a couple of minutes, Hattie Belle again wiped away her tears with her napkin, and asked in a voice that could barely be heard, "And Lemmie?"

Ella's dark eyes showed surprise. "Why I thought you'd probably read about Lem. He's fine. In the Navy section, at the back of one of our Boston paper, it said, 'The *Scorpion* sailed from Havana for Tompkinsville, Nov. 27.'"

"Oh! He wrote that he was going to leave before Thanksgiving. But he left after—on Sunday, the second day of our gale. The storm would have left the Caribbean days before it got here. He's safe! It's such wonderful news I can hardly believe it!" Hattie Belle smiled through tears of relief. "I'd had such a terrible dream about the *Scorpion* that I was sure you'd come to tell me she'd sunk."

"Oh, no, Hattie Belle! I'm so sorry you thought that! When Uncle Eph said someone should let you know what was going on, Ozias and I looked at each other, and started getting our outdoor clothes together."

"That was so kind of you!" Hattie Belle said.

"We wanted to do it—partly for you and partly for ourselves. There was so much worrying and crying going on we were glad to leave."

"Now if only we could read good news about the others," Hattie Belle said.

She heard the side door open, and Ozias and her father came in to get warm, drink some hot coffee, and have a bite to eat.

After Ella and her brother left, Lemmie's letter kept running through her mind. When she thought of the page about the parrot, Jocko, and imagined him swearing at the preacher in Spanish, she smiled to herself.

The next afternoon, one of the papers reported: "Scorpion arrived at Port Royal." After she read it, she danced around the kitchen. Lemmie was really all right! He was sailing up the coast toward New York.

The following day, Lemmie's vessel was mentioned again: "Scorpion sailed from Port Royal for Tompkinsville."

"Listen to this, Papa!" she said, but he was reading the names of newly found wrecks to Mary, who was making a mince pie, and he didn't hear.

"Oh, great!" her father suddenly cried out.

Mary stopped rolling out pie crust and turned to ask, "What does it say, Will?"

"It's about the *Chamberlain*! It says, 'The schooner weathered the terrific gale safely, her only loss being the forestay sails and a yawl boat. She arrived at Vineyard Haven, preceded to anchor and will proceed."

"Wonderful news!" Mary said.

"Yes, wonderful," Hattie Belle echoed, but her mind was on Lemmie and the *Scorpion*, sailing toward New York.

She tried again to tell them about Lemmie, but they were so busy talking about the *Chamberlain* that she couldn't get in a word.

While she waited, in a glow of happiness, for a break in the conversation, she glanced down at the *Lincoln County News*. In the middle of the front page, the word *Scorpion* caught her eye. She read, "Anxiety for the United States gunboat Scorpion, which has not been heard from since Sunday, when she was supposed to have left Havana." That was all—no more. Her heart began to pound.

"Look Papa," she cried. "It says here the *Scorpion* hasn't been heard from since Sunday, when she was supposed to have left Havana. But the Boston paper says the *Scorpion* sailed from Port Royal for Tompkinsville. What does 'supposed to have left' mean? Have the Boston reports been a mistake? Do you think a reporter mixed up the names of two ships coming home from the war?"

Captain Davis nodded. "Might be. The Lincoln County paper doesn't have reporters, so it probably came from the Navy."

"So that would be the right one," Hattie Belle said in a voice that could barely be heard.

"We don't know that for sure."

Hattie Belle thought about her dream, in which she had seen Lemmie on board the *Scorpion*, caught in the trough of the sea.

She pulled his letter out of her apron pocket and squinted hard at the blurry cancellation at the top of the envelope. As she painstakingly picked out the letters and numbers, she became quite sure it had been mailed on November 21 from Havana. He had written it before he left Cuba. She wondered if he'd died in the hurricane she'd seen in her dream—not the one just here, but a second one to come up from the Gulf of Mexico. The letter might be from a dead man.

Chapter 16

Crossing the Bar

The snow glistened in the sun, and icicles hung from the roof like frozen tears.

Zena, looking thinner than ever in her black dress, sat in the rocking chair by the window, holding her Bible on her lap. Joe hadn't spoken all morning. He sat on the deacon's bench, in front of the hearth, staring into the red and yellow flames.

Josie, in her Gibson Girl shirt and skirt, couldn't sit still, but moved constantly about the kitchen, wiping off the window sills, where the storm had leaked in, sweeping the floor, scrubbing the oil cloth covered table where she had made biscuits, and talking endlessly.

As she handed her mother a cup of tea and a buttered biscuit, she asked for what seemed the hundredth time. "Do you think Uncle Frank and Aunt Delia can really be gone? Their names haven't been in the newspapers. Maybe one of them got sick, and at the last minute they couldn't leave."

"Maybe, child, but not likely."

"How about Percy, Mother? Don't you think he's all right? You know how quick he is. If the *Addie E.* had washed ashore at Race Point, he would have jumped off and fought his way up to higher ground."

"You know as much as I do, child. All we know is what the papers said."

"I think they still don't realize that the schooner the reporter wrote about was not the *Addie E. Snow*. I think Percy is somewhere in safe harbor."

"I hope you're right, Josie."

The girl was sweeping the floor again, hard and fast. She paused in front of her mother. "What do you think it means when the newspapers say there is concern for the gunboat *Scorpion*, that the navy has lost all touch with her? I think she was caught in one of those tropical hurricanes, that start down there, and the men are waiting out the gale on one of the islands. There's no reason to think the ship is lost."

"I hope you're right."

"How about Lawrence and Myrtie Belle, Mother?" Her voice was high pitched now—almost a scream. "I prayed they would make it to the safety of Salem harbor. Now that I know how hard hit it was—with most of the ships wrecked or thrown up on the rocks, I wish I hadn't." She began vigorously dusting the sideboard, with long sweeping strokes. "Do you think the *Robert A.* was wrecked? Do you think Lawrence and Myrtie Belle are all right?"

"We don't know yet, child, we don't know, but I'm sure your prayers did them nothing but good."

A look of relief came into the girl's eyes.

Joe, who hadn't touched the cup of coffee or biscuit Josie had laid in front of him, now rose stiffly, and mumbled, "Going to the post office to wait for the mail."

"I'm well enough to go, too," Josie said. "I'm not sick anymore." She glanced at her mother, who seemed not to hear her.

Zena was reading from the book of Job, whispering the words: "'For the thing which I greatly feared is come upon me, and that which I was afraid of is come unto me.'"

Josie quickly put on her cloak, boots, and muffler and followed her father out the door.

The little post office was crowded, but quiet, none of the usual small talk. When the mail carrier came in, those who were waiting shuffled about, their faces tense.

When the postmaster pushed Joe's mail through the window, Josie spotted a letter in Delia's handwriting. In what seemed like one motion, she grabbed it and tore open the envelope. "Aunt Delia and Uncle Frank are alive!" she cried, eyes alight with joy. "They missed the sailing! Didn't I tell you that's what happened? Didn't I tell you?" As Joe, in a kind of daze, moved away from the window, she danced along at his side.

"Look! Look!" she cried, as her eyes fell upon the mail her father had picked up. "A letter from Lemmie, too!" Plucking it out of her father's hand, she tore it open. "Hurray! He's in Port Royal, North Carolina, and just fine."

"Praise God!" Joe said.

"The *Scorpion* is in port for repairs. They were in one of those tropical hurricanes—didn't I tell you?—when a great wave slammed across the deck, and smashed the wheel. He says here, 'In an instant, the ship fell into the trough. But another fellow and I were able to mend the wheel in a hurry. Using halyards torn from the flagstaff, we fastened two iron jacking bars to its hub. The ship came up right away, but the gale went on for 24 hours, and we bailed all night with buckets. In the morning the storm began to wear itself out, and later in the day, we made Port Royal, thankful to be alive.'"

"He says here at the end, 'Will you do up my good shirt, and press my suit and vest? I want to get married as soon as I'm mustered out and the train can get me home.'

"Oh, I knew he was all right! I knew it! I hope Hattie Belle knows too."

Joe, unable to say a word, stood with tears running down his lined cheeks.

After giving him a hug, Josie said, "I can go faster than you, Father, so I'm going to run home ahead of you and show Mother these letters. She'll be so happy!"

He watched through the window as she raced up the road. Could it be that the family's bad luck was changing? He noticed that his cousin, Elmer Fitch, came into the post office, and stood at the mail window, on the other side of the room. Usually Joe would have called out to him, but today he just nodded, as their eyes met. He'd tell Elmer the good news later. Right now there were too many people between them, and he felt too drained to talk.

"Hold on there," the postmaster called, as Joe started out the door. "There's another letter for you here."

The writing on the front was identical to that on Lemmie's letter, but it had been mailed from Salem, so it had to be from Lawrence. He went back to where he and Josie had stood, and tore open the envelope. After scanning the letter, he sat down on the bench for a few minutes, then stood up slowly, walked out of the building on unsteady legs, and headed toward home.

"Want a ride, Joe?" Elmer shouted from his buggy.

No answer.

"Bad news, Joe?"

When there was still no answer, the cousin drove slowly by, but looked back several times.

Too tired to climb the rise of Wawenock Ridge, Joe rested in the front yard, leaning against a tree near the road which had lost its branches in the storm. Zena and Josie saw him from the window, and throwing on their cloaks and boots, ran out to help him.

Inside, he sank down on the old deacon's bench, gave Zena a long look, and pulled the letter from his pocket.

"Oh, wonderful!" Josie cried, looking at the envelope. "It's from Lawrence. Didn't I tell you everything is all right?"

"Everything's not all right," Joe said, speaking with effort.

The girl looked alarmed. "Was Myrtic Belle hurt in the storm? Has the schooner been wrecked?"

He shook his head, but said nothing.

Josie pulled the letter out of the envelope, gave it to her mother, then stood behind the rocking chair so she could read it at the same time.

"Dear Folks,

"I don't know how to write this letter. All I can think of is to begin by telling you the *Robert A.* wasn't loaded as soon as promised, so we didn't make it here to Salem before the heavy weather hit. We stayed out the storm at Hyannis. Myrtie, who'd been seasick, decided to go by train from there back to our place in Rockland.

"When I arrived at Salem, I found Captain Richard Snow waiting for me. He said he had received word that the medicine chest cover of the *Addie E. Snow* had washed ashore and been found by the Lighthouse Keeper at Race Point, half buried in the sand, among wreckage from the *Portland.*"

"No!" Zena said. "No!" She blinked back tears, so she could continue.

"I just stood there dumbfounded. Captain Richard said the authorities had sent for him to come to Race Point and make legal identification. He said he thought I'd want to go with him."

"Oh Lord," Zena moaned, wiping her eyes. "Oh Lord."

"Percy must have ripped the medicine chest cover off and thrown it overboard the way Snow captains are trained to do when they're in trouble—lost, and think they're not going to make it. The hope is that someone will find the cover, with the schooner's name on it and send help.

"We left the Robert A. Snow at Salem, and took a cab through rain for the station. After we arrived at Race Point, we found Lighthouse Keeper Harvender in his damaged living quarters, his windows broken by the gale. He looked grim and tired as he looked for the medicine chest cover, then handed it to us without a word.

"It seemed as if I could barely stand it to see that cover I knew so well, with it's fancy scroll work, and the gold letters that spell out ADDIE E. SNOW.

"When I asked to see where the cover had been found, Keeper Harvender led us along the water's edge, with its broken wharves, and beaches piled with wreckage from destroyed vessels.

"'The Portland went down not far from here,' Keeper Harvender said. 'We'll soon come to her wreckage. More has come in today. The captain of the life saving station thought the wind change could cause the wreckage that may have been drifting south to return to the coast.

"'I don't know what else from the *Addie E.* you might find. I think anything of worth may have been taken.' He told us that during this morning's gale, the beach was dotted with wagons, whose drivers were bent on stealing trunks and other valuables that washed ashore. Because the rain was coming down in buckets there wasn't much the surfmen could do to stop the thieves.

"Farther down the beach, we stopped at a place where wreckage from the *Portland* had washed in. I remember seeing an empty ice cream can, a life preserver, clothing and bed clothing.

"'It was right around here that I found the medicine chest cover,' Keeper Harvender said.

"He and Captain Richard and I began looking among the various items, slipping about as we walked, on the great number of fish that had washed in. 'Strange,' the Keeper said, as he almost fell, 'red snappers never come this far north.'"

"Red snappers!" Zena gasped. "Percy's fish."

Josie leaned over to take her mother's hand. It was hard to go on reading the letter, but after a minute or two, they did.

"As we were searching, I heard a shout from a young boy, who had come out on the beach with his friends to look around. 'Look there!' he cried, 'Look there!' I turned and saw what appeared to be a toy boat sailing in toward shore. As I stepped out into the water, she landed at my feet.

I picked her up and saw it was the little model of the *Addie E.* that I'd carved for Percy."

"Oh no!" Josie cried. "Oh no!"

"Percy's gone, isn't he Joe?" Zena said.

He nodded slowly.

The next page began,

"I knew then there was no hope. Captain Richard and I will return to Salem by train and take the Robert A. back to Rockland. Then Myrtie and I will head for Walpole. I would like to have a family service to mark Percy's passing, the way we did when we lost Frank. If that is what you would like, Myrtie and I will do all the work. I'll clean and she'll cook. She'll bring one of her instruments, too, the violin, most likely. I know she'll play whatever old hymns you'd like her to, and I'll read 'Crossing the Bar.'

We'll see you soon,
With all our love,
Lawrence and Myrtie."

"I want to be alone," Josie sobbed, as she rushed into the hall, and up the stairs to her room.

Zena got up and walked slowly toward the pantry, where she stood in front of the black iron sink, and looked out the window at the special beauty of the day's end. The tall pointed trees along the river were silhouetted against a red and yellow sky.

She heard uneven footsteps, and Joe came to stand beside her.

"Sunset," Zena whispered, and although they hadn't known they were going to, they began repeating together, the mariner's eulogy.

"Sunset and evening star,

And one clear call for me!

And may there be no moaning of the bar,

When I put out to sea...."

They stayed at the window, leaning against each other, until the sunset faded into the darkness and only the evening star remained.

Model of the ADDIE E. SNOW
by Capt. Lawrence Brown

Acknowledgements

My mother, Emily Brown Stone, daughter of Captain Lemuel Brown and Hattie Belle, provided the inspiration for this book with her stories of her seafaring family. She hopes the old schooners days, which were both romantic and tragic, will never be forgotten.

Heartfelt appreciation goes to daughter Martha Daniels, who over a period of years, read, corrected, and encouraged my efforts to write a book that would have meaning to those who come later.

Many, many thanks go to Aunt Mary Brown Strahan, my mother's sister, and the keeper of family records and pictures. Her recollections, plus photographs, letters, and memorabilia from the last century have given the book's characters a solid reality

Virginia Brown Whitney, daughter of Captain Lawrence and Myrtie Belle, has been a knowledgeable and helpful companion as we visited ancestors' homes, one room schools, and cemeteries then searched for family records in town, county, and state offices.

Much gratitude goes to Phyllis Arth, a dear friend and talented researcher, who found magazines published in 1898, reports of the Spanish War in Cuba, maps and articles about old Boston; even the Boston City Directory listing Uncle Frank Stevens.

I've depended on Aunt Dorothy Brown, daughter-in-law of Captain Lemuel and Hattie Belle, as an historian, well versed in the Pemaquid Harbor of a hundred years ago; and as a naturalist, knowledgeable about its flora and fauna.

My many thanks go to Bertram Snow, whose great grandfather owned the I.L. Snow Company of Rockland, Maine, for giving me a tour of the shipyard; explanations about the marine railway; and the timing of the sad visit to Cape Cod's Race Point.

Jane Tucker, Wiscasset historian, took time from her own writing to send shipping news clippings about the four Captains Brown—the return of one from Russia, after being rescued from a sinking schooner, and the deaths of two at sea.

Jane Spofford, granddaughter of Captain Lemuel and Hattie Belle, always alert to my needs, sent histories of Pemaquid, notice of available vital records of old Bristol, Stevens records from Captain Lemuel's Bible, and a cookbook of recipes from the past.

I'm grateful for the help of Lemuel Brown, our grandfather's namesake, who at my request read the entire manuscript to make sure my portrayal of Down East customs and beliefs at the turn of the last century ring true.

Son John Melton has provided on-going assistance by going with me on extensive fact finding trips, taking pictures of main characters and captains' favorite vessels, and giving unending help with the computer.

Son Jim Melton accompanied me to the National Archives and Library of Congress to discover the log of the *Scorpion* from 1898, and a "Marine

Note of Protest," written in Libau, Russia, and signed by Captain Lemuel after the loss of the *Sheepscot*.

Noel Brassey sent me the big picture of her grandmother Josie Brown, taken when she was a girl, so I might copy it for this book. She also let me copy from the "Stevens Bible" which is a thick album filled with photos of Zena Brown's people from Pemaquid.

My thanks go to William Hoffman for his excellent and perceptive critiques.

Without the understanding and constant support of my husband, George, whose contributions would take several pages to list, this book could not have been written.

ABOUT THE AUTHOR

Mary Melton grew up listening to stories of the sea, and of her mother's seafaring people in Down East Maine. Following many years as a journalist, she began work on the book her mother asked her to write—about the days of the two and three masted schooners—before they were forgotten. Looking back on growing up, the happiest times were summers in Pemaquid Harbor. She and her husband, the parents of five grown children, live in Virginia and spend time each year in Maine, following the footsteps of her ancestors.